General Education Essentials

General Education Essentials

A Guide for College Faculty

Paul Hanstedt

Foreword by Terrel L. Rhodes

Association
of American
Colleges and
Universities

JOSSEY-BASS
A Wiley Imprint
www.josseybass.com

Published by Jossey-Bass
A Wiley Imprint
989 Market Street, San Francisco, CA 94103-1741—www.josseybass.com

Credits are continued on page 165.

Jossey-Bass books and products are available through most bookstores. To contact Jossey-Bass directly call our Customer Care Department within the U.S. at 800-956-7739, outside the U.S. at 317-572-3986, or fax 317-572-4002.

Wiley also publishes its books in a variety of electronic formats and by print-on-demand. Not all content that is available in standard print versions of this book may appear or be packaged in all book formats. If you have purchased a version of this book that did not include media that is referenced by or accompanies a standard print version, you may request this media by visiting http://booksupport.wiley.com. For more information about Wiley products, visit us www.wiley.com.

Library of Congress Cataloging-in-Publication Data

Hanstedt, Paul, date
  General education essentials : a guide for college faculty / Paul Hanstedt ;
foreword by Terrel L. Rhodes.
       p. cm. — (The Jossey-Bass higher and adult education series)
  Includes bibliographical references and index.
  ISBN 978-1-118-32185-0 (pbk.); 978-1-118-32953-5 (ebk);
978-1-118-32954-2 (ebk); 978-1-118-32955-9 (ebk)
1. Universities and colleges—Curricula—United States.—Planning. 2.
General education—United States. I. Title.
  LB2361.5H36 2012
  378.1′99—dc23

                                                                2012004824

Printed in the United States of America
FIRST EDITION

PB Printing   10 9 8 7 6 5 4 3 2 1

The Jossey-Bass
Higher and Adult Education Series

Association of American Colleges and Universities

AAC&U is the leading national association concerned with the quality, vitality, and public standing of undergraduate liberal education. Its members are committed to extending the advantages of a liberal education to all students, regardless of academic specialization or intended career. Founded in 1915, AAC&U now comprises more than 1,250 member institutions—including accredited public and private colleges, community colleges, and universities of every type and size.

AAC&U organizes its work around five broad goals:

- A Guiding Vision for Liberal Education
- Inclusive Excellence
- Intentional and Integrative Learning
- Civic, Diversity, and Global Engagement
- Authentic Evidence

Through its publications, meetings, public advocacy, and programs, AAC&U provides a powerful voice for liberal education. AAC&U works to reinforce the commitment to liberal education at both the national and the local level and to help individual colleges and universities keep the quality of student learning at the core of their work as they evolve to meet new economic and social challenges. With a nearly one-hundred-year history and national stature, AAC&U is an influential catalyst for educational improvement and reform.

AAC&U has worked intensively on the issue of general education reform since the early 1980s. AAC&U general education initiatives aim to ensure that every undergraduate student experiences a relevant and challenging general education curriculum. In addition to working with campuses to strengthen their general education programs overall or to reform specific aspects of them (e.g. science requirements or diversity requirements), AAC&U initiatives address strengthening general education for transfer students, embedding high expectations and meaningful assessment of student learning, and general education as essential for enhancing curricula and pedagogy. Every year, AAC&U sponsors a spring meeting on General Education and Assessment in February and a summer institute for campus teams on the same topic in June.

For information about all of AAC&U's resources, see: www.aacu.org

CONTENTS

FOREWORD

As a twenty-five-year-plus faculty member, it was a pleasure to read *General Education Essentials;* I wish I had such a resource when I began my university teaching career. Of course I had been an undergraduate student, so I knew what general education was, what a major meant, electives, and so forth, but I had no idea that there actually were concepts and theories that underlay and justified general education as an important, integral part of a quality undergraduate education. I thought that general education was a set of courses students were required to take so we would be exposed to all the areas traditionally associated with being a well-rounded, educated person. Therefore, as a faculty member I simply had to teach my introductory course as I always did; students could take the course and learn about the basics of American government and be much better persons as a result. Little did I know at the time.

Paul Hanstedt has a deft touch in crafting this book on general education—that too-often least-valued part of an undergraduate education. Before students enter college they are told in a variety of ways that general education is something to "get out the way" as soon as possible in order to get on to the really important part of their education—the major. Hanstedt, though, manages to bring to bear the latest research on the purposes and impact of general education for student learning and a whole set of practical examples and approaches to teaching general education classes that, together, hold the potential to improve faculty pedagogy and students' undergraduate experience. As a long-time faculty member with both domestic and international teaching experience in large and small colleges, Hanstedt draws upon his experience in multiple environments for his insights into reformulating general education. As a literature and writing professor, he brings an ease with language and an ability to describe and portray general education as a living and breathing integral part of the preparation of students for success in a complex world of change; a world that also requires our approach to and representation of general education to change as well.

As the author points out early in this book, change in what we mean by general education has happened: "Indeed, the rate of change is such that some would argue the main title of this book is inaccurate: it's not 'general' education we're after anymore, a term many associate with 'breadth' and that evolves from Enlightenment and Victorian era ideas about what makes a person cultured. These days, more often than not, the term of choice is *liberal education*, indicating not a left-leaning slant to scholarly thinking but a sense of what it means to create liberated human beings—people who are independent and flexible in their thinking and capable of responding to the demands of a changing world in civic-minded, deliberative ways." The need for change has become an alarm for many.

At a time when numerous reports from academics and the media are calling for change because U.S. students are not performing at the same levels as students in other parts of the world, especially in several Asian countries, many of those same countries are looking to the U.S. system of higher education as the answer to the shortcomings in their own graduates as identified by the business leaders in their own countries. Hong Kong, Japan, and Korea are all introducing general education into their baccalaureate degree programs because they believe that general education provides U.S.-educated students with the creative and integrative skills their own students lack—skills essential to be competitive in a rapidly changing world economy that demands more versatile and innovative abilities than they are finding among their own country's college graduates.

Not only does this book present a cogent argument for the central role general education plays in an undergraduate's education; it also deconstructs what this more sophisticated and useful conception of liberal education means for faculty who are engaged in teaching the courses that comprise general education programs across the country. It is still the case that preparation of new faculty in graduate programs usually contains nothing about general education, liberal education, or the critical role they can and need to play in a student's higher education. Nothing prepares new faculty to understand what it means to teach a course included in the general education program and how it needs to be different from a course that primarily serves as an introduction to a content area. Nor is there anything in graduate preparation of faculty to suggest that general education courses shouldn't be only introductory courses. Advanced courses, including capstone courses, can be and need to be part of a general education program if students are to develop the skills and abilities necessary for success.

In this concise guide for college faculty, readers will encounter a cogent argument for a contemporary liberal education—the big picture—followed by an examination of the courses that often comprise the curriculum of general education, and finally a look at the critical importance of the assignment in achieving the purposes of a reconceived program. A third to a quarter of most undergraduate curricula is composed of general education requirements, yet to hear my faculty colleagues discuss general education, its primary role is to expose students to the breadth of knowledge associated with the well-rounded, educated person. This is an outdated and unexamined notion that ignores both the fact that today's students have no problem having access and exposure to an incredibly broad array of knowledge and content, and the recognition that having students take a collection of mostly introductory courses does little to enhance a student's educational understanding of important disciplines, traditions, and intercultural or civic understanding beyond being able to answer television game show questions.

In Part Two, the author moves beyond the theoretical and conceptual basis for liberal education and provides strategies and a rationale for designing courses and building intentional programs of study within a general education program. General education is a program of study not unlike disciplinary or interdisciplinary majors. The author argues that general education deserves the same attention and consideration as any organized field of study. Indeed, general education does much of the heavy lifting in grounding and building the essential learning outcomes that both faculty and employers have firmly concluded are necessary for student success as citizens and employees.[1] To illustrate the arguments for an intentional approach to general education, the author provides examples of colleges and universities that have been successfully establishing coherent general education programs.

In Part Three, the author turns his attention to two of the book's most important components of powerful general education programs—assignments and assessment. Research on student learning and pedagogy has concluded that a significant reason students often do not demonstrate learning around particular topics or issues is because they were not clearly asked to demonstrate the desired learning. In other words, the assignment was not constructed in such a way that it asked for demonstration of the learning being expected by

---

[1] *College Learning for the New Global Century.* 2007. Washington, D.C.: Association of American Colleges and Universities.

the instructor. Teaching and learning centers across the country have been stressing to faculty the importance of developing clear and focused assignments for many years.

Coupled with the reconsideration of assignments to enhance learning, the emergence of new approaches to assessment have begun to reinforce the usefulness of assessments that can provide evidence of student learning, or its lack, that faculty members can actually use to improve their classroom pedagogy and effectiveness. Assessment no longer needs to be something that is imposed from the outside for accountability reporting, but is becoming a valuable teaching resource for enhancing student learning and faculty success. Campus-level evidence is emerging of the positive usefulness and impact of good assessment.[2]

General Education Essentials does what previous books on general education have not been able to do. This book manages to provide a compelling theoretical framework for the principles and practices of liberal education necessary for college graduates in the twenty-first century; to connect the theory to examples of faculty-led implementation on different types of campuses; and to do so in a style and manner that is readable and useful for the typical faculty member who may have limited exposure to or interest in general education. Full-time and part-time faculty in any discipline and at any size campus with any type of mission can pick up this volume and learn something that will help her or him improve teaching and learning. If an entire campus embraced the contents of this book, their general education program could be transformed and the performance of their students enhanced.

I wish I had had this book when I was starting my own teaching career. I would have been a better teacher, and my students would have been better prepared for life after college.

Terrel L. Rhodes
Vice President for Curriculum, Quality, and Assessment
Association of American Colleges and Universities

---

[2]"Assessing Liberal Education Outcomes Through VALUE Rubrics." *Peer Review.* Fall/Winter 2012. Association of American Colleges and Universities.

ABOUT THE AUTHOR

Paul Hanstedt is Professor of English at Roanoke College in Salem, Virginia. During his tenure there as director of general education, he led his campus in a successful curricular revision that resulted in a theme-based general education program featuring writing, quantitative reasoning, and oral communications across the curriculum. The corecipient of a half-million-dollar grant from the Fund for the Improvement of Postsecondary Education for sustainable faculty development, Hanstedt also received a Fulbright to spend a year in Hong Kong as part of a team supporting the universities there as they designed and implemented general education programs. In addition to his work in curricular, course, and faculty development, he is an active writer of fiction and nonfiction, recently publishing *Hong Konged,* a memoir of his year in Asia with his three children under the age of ten.

ACKNOWLEDGMENTS

I must begin by expressing my gratitude to the Fulbright organization, as well as to Po Chung, without whom my time in Hong Kong and this subsequent book would not have been possible. Similarly, many thanks go to Tom Osgood, Glenn Shive, and the people on the ground at the Hong Kong America Center who made it all work.

My thinking in matters of general education (and otherwise) has been invaluably shaped by my Fulbright colleagues that year: David Campion, Joe Chaney, Janel Curry, Hedley Freake, Gray Kocchar-Lindgren, and David Pong. In particular, I owe a debt of gratitude to Hedley Freake, who first pointed out to me the idea that curricular models are not either-or but rather exist on a continuum. After that, everything began to fall into place.

I also acknowledge the support of Roanoke College, my home institution, particularly its wise and patient president, Mike Maxey. In addition I owe a great deal to various faculty and administrators, past and present, for their support: John Day, Michael Hakkenberg, Richard Smith, Adrienne Bloss, Susan Kirby, Sabine O'Hara, Katherine Hoffman, Gail Steehler, Chris Lee, Robert Schultz, Wendy Larson-Harris, Chris Buchholz, and many, many others, without whom my understanding of general education would be greatly diminished. Thanks also go to Dan Johnson of Washington and Lee University, whose wisdom in the field of psychology was invaluable to me throughout this project.

I thank the administration, faculty, and staff of the Hong Kong Institute of Education. My time there taught me a lot about the complexities of developing and implementing a sophisticated curricular model. In particular, I thank President Anthony B. L. Cheung, Professor C. C. Lam, Dr. K. S. Lee, Dr. William Sin, Dr. Huixian Xu, Dr. Iris Kam, Elaine Cheng, Nana Lai, Tracy Yeung, and the infinitely wise and gracious Dr. Anita Kit Wa Chan. Additional thanks go to Dr. Christopher Deneen, of Hong Kong University, and Dr. Gavin T. L. Brown, of the University of Auckland, for their constant support, complete unwillingness to settle for easy answers, and slightly off-kilter perspectives on what is and is not funny.

Many thanks as well go to the Association of American Colleges and Universities, particularly Debra Humphreys and David Tritelli, for their support of this project and my work more broadly.

I conclude by pointing to four scholars and writers whose work has influenced my own efforts in the classroom, on the page, and in workshops. Pretty much any time I discuss matters of course design, I am thinking about the work of Barbara Tewksbury, whose approach to course design is a model of common sense; in addition, James Zull, whose book *The Art of Changing the Brain* helped me understand the biological basis for learning; James Bean, whose *Engaging Ideas* has become a bible for all who are interested in writing- and thinking-across-the-curriculum; and Jerry Gaff, whose "Avoiding the Pot- holes: Strategies for Reforming General Education" has influenced everyone working with curricular reform in liberal education for the past thirty years. Anyone interested in making sense of an academy overwhelmed by changing expectations, tightening budgets, and myriad social and political forces intent on reshaping the university will find comfort, insight, and clarity in the work of these four scholars.

Finally, my love and thanks to Ellen and the kids for being kind and reminding me of what matters.

General Education Essentials

INTRODUCTION

Perhaps it's best to begin by stating the obvious: today's faculty are busier than ever before. In the past few decades, research and publication expectations at universities at most B.A.-, M.A.-, and Ph.D.-granting institutions have gone up. Teaching loads, by contrast, have not gone down. Indeed, with tighter budgets, chances are that faculty will see more students, not fewer, in their classrooms. And with new initiatives ranging from assessment to diversity to green campuses, the degree to which faculty are expected to serve on departmental and university committees, advise students, and perform other forms of service has generally risen.

In addition, lately academia seems to be taking its cues from corporate America and embracing paradigm shift at a dizzying rate. Every year it seems that the administration comes to the faculty with a new catchphrase, an altered mission focus, a new five-year plan. It's not uncommon for faculty facing an institutional discussion of "curricular change," "curricular revision," "core development," "general education," "liberal education," or "integrative learning" to find themselves groaning inwardly and thinking, *Oh, no. Here we go again.*

Or maybe not. Maybe some of us—graduates of liberal arts institutions perhaps, or those in a field that embraces interdisciplinarity, or maybe just those who are broadly curious—have a different response. These folks may remember with fondness the startling realization they had in a required class outside their intended major, or the spark of connection they experienced

1

when they understood that what was happening in the mathematics class and the philosophy class were not so very different.

In the end, it probably doesn't matter how we respond, intellectually or emotionally, to the possibility of curricular change because chances are, it's going to happen. Every year the American Association of Colleges and Universities hosts a general education workshop, offering teams of faculty the opportunity to spend five nights in eight-by-twelve cinderblock dorm rooms and five days discussing curricular revision with their colleagues and experts in the field. And every year universities from all over the world have their applications declined because there isn't space to accommodate everyone who is interested.

The reasons for this surge in interest in curricular revision are many and are covered in detail in Chapter One. Suffice it to say, though, that much of it has to do with the recognition that the world is changing dramatically and quickly and that the old ways of doing things might not be effective enough anymore. Indeed, the rate of change is such that some would argue that the title of this book is inaccurate: it's not "general" education we're after anymore, a term many associate with breadth and that evolved from Enlightenment and Victorian era ideas about what makes a person cultured. These days, more often than not, the term of choice is *liberal education*, indicating not a left-leaning slant to scholarly thinking but a sense of what it means to create liberated human beings—people who are independent and flexible in their thinking and capable of responding to the demands of a changing world in civic-minded, deliberative ways.

So what does this mean for the people who teach the classes, serve on the committees, and do the scheduling for the next term and the term after that? Quite a bit, actually: it means new opportunities and new challenges. It means lots of discussions with colleagues in their own and other departments; it means some heated debates, some anxieties, and some new insights that may cause us to look at our work and our students in different ways.

Most of all, though, it means something of a learning curve. There are new terms, new assumptions (often counterintuitive), new data, new methodologies. And while we'd like to think that university faculty would by nature be inclined toward lifelong learning and adaptation to change, when it comes to engaging in an entirely new way of thinking about our work, some of us may be resistant. Perhaps it's because we're so busy or bound to tradition but as one scholar pointed out at a workshop I once attended, "Statistically faculty are more likely to leave their spouses than change institutions." In short, we like our jobs the way they are.

The purpose of this book is not necessarily to alleviate any anxieties we might have about general education, liberal education, or curricular change, though that would be a nice by-product. Rather, I designed and wrote this book to give a quick introduction to current trends in general education reform, as well as a sense of its implications for our work, particularly in the classroom.

General Education Essentials: A Guide for College Faculty is divided into three parts, moving from macro to micro. The titles of each part pretty much speak for themselves. Part One, ''The Big Picture,'' discusses curricular design overall, the trends and options, and why general education is evolving the way it is.

Part Two, ''General Education at the Course Level,'' looks at the implications of this evolution for our work in the classroom: how will it affect syllabi, content, what we do and don't cover in the classroom? As with Part One, Part Two consists first of these ideas in the abstract and then offers several illustrations designed to clarify and spark instructor thinking.

Part Three, ''General Education at the Assignment and Assessment Level,'' is slightly less symmetrical. It too begins with a discussion in the abstract of the implications of current general education trends for the types of work we ask our students to do. I offer multiple examples in multiple fields exploring some of the techniques we might use to ensure that students are gaining the skills they need to be insightful scholars and productive citizens. Chapter Six, ''The Chapter You May Want to Skip: Institutional Assessment and General Education,'' may at first seem like a departure from a microfocus on the classroom, but perhaps university assessment should be driven by what happens in the classroom rather than the other way around.

As is perhaps clear by now, what follows is by no means an exhaustive discussion of general education; rather, the emphasis is on giving faculty enough information to get them into the conversation. Beyond that, I've assumed that because we're all scholars, readers who are interested in a particular topic will take the time to do further research.

Chapter One is essential for understanding the shift from distributive to integrative models of general education, but readers can pick and choose among the chapters depending on their particular need and the degree to which they want abstract theories (Chapters One, Three, and the first section of Chapter Five), or specific curricular ideas for implementation (Chapters Two, Four, and Six and the later sections of Chapter Five).

GENERAL EDUCATION AND ITS RELATION TO THE MAJOR

When I first led a curricular revision on my own campus, I made the announcement that whatever the specifics of the curricular model we developed would be, it should in no way have any impact on the majors at my college. My thinking at this point, I'll confess, was fairly cynical. As is the case at many other campuses, curricular revision at Roanoke College was a touchy subject.

Faculty were worried about how it might affect their teaching, their workload, their majors, their time for research. It was my sense that by drawing a very clear demarcation between the majors and general education, we could ease faculty anxieties about the former and aid the progress of the latter.

In retrospect, I think this was an unproductive decision. I say this not because I now believe that general education should be allowed to reshape majors and other programs. Rather, I wish I'd kept the conversation about general education and its relationship to the major going because separating the two may limit the ability of general education to aid the major in creating better graduates. Allow me to explain what I mean by this. There are many who assume general education works as shown in Figure I.1.

In this model, "general education" is assumed to encompass simple foundational skills that, once gained, will enable students to do the "real" work. (I've actually heard this term used, at several institutions on several continents.) I understand something of the impulse behind this way of thinking. It's nice to imagine that someone else can teach our students "basic" skills before they get to the major, relieving us of that duty and allowing our courses to pursue more high-end work.

Unfortunately, this approach fails to acknowledge something that most faculty experience nearly daily: just because a student has learned something in his first year doesn't mean he'll remember it in his advanced classes. The brain isn't a lockbox that holds every piece of information it encounters, providing easy access when retrieval is appropriate. Rather, as a biologist friend puts it, the brain operates more like a use-it-or-lose-it circuit board, creating strong neural networks when information is applied regularly and allowing unused networks to fade into nearly irretrievable obscurity.

Then there's the fact that many of the skills we consider basic and foundational aren't really that. Ronald Kellogg, a University of St. Louis psychologist who studies writing, asserts that the kinds of expository work we ask our students to do is akin to becoming an expert violinist or chess player, requiring a minimum of five thousand hours of solitary practice simply to rise above the

First Year	General Education
Second Year	
Third Year	Major
Fourth Year	

Figure I.1. General Education as Foundational

level of amateur (2008). As much as we may like to believe that a required first-year course in writing (or math or oral communications or anything else) exonerates us from ever having to teach these skills in our major courses, the fact is that such an approach will likely leave both us and our students disappointed and frustrated.

Perhaps a better way to think about general education in relation to the major looks something like the model in Figures I.2 and I.3. In both of these models, general education runs throughout a four-year curriculum. As a result, several things occur:

- Students have the opportunity to develop the skills associated with contemporary general education throughout their time at college.
- Consequently, having repeated practice with these skills at increasingly complex and intellectually demanding levels, students will have a better chance of learning them.
- Also consequently, majors will benefit by having students arrive in their classes more practiced in these essential ways of thinking.

Some would argue that some of the skills in question should be taught in the majors, not in general education. And indeed they should be: reinforcing skills like critical thinking and quantitative reasoning in a student's major,

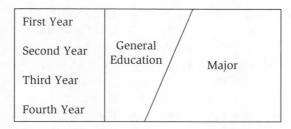

First Year		
Second Year	General Education	Major
Third Year		
Fourth Year		

Figure I.2. General Education and the Major: An Alternative Perspective

First Year		
Second Year	General Education	Major
Third Year		
Fourth Year		

Figure I.3. General Education and the Major: Another Alternative Perspective

where intrinsic motivation is likely to be higher, not only provides students with added practice in these areas but hammers home the point that these skills matter; they're not just some stuff that some committee somewhere decided was good for students. But to think that majors can carry the burden for teaching these skills on their own ignores the reality that content in most fields is growing at an exponential rate, making absolute coverage increasingly difficult, if not impossible. (More on this in Chapter One.)

Indeed, as Schilling and Smith (2010) point out, it's not uncommon to find increasing emphasis on the goals of liberal education in many professional programs such as business, engineering, and nursing. Concordia University in Montreal, for example, has developed its General Studies to augment programs, intent on ensuring that students in engineering and computer science learn concepts and practices traditionally aligned with the liberal arts. Since its creation in 2004, the General Studies Unit at Concordia has worked to develop ways to have students explore "notions of professionalism and ethics, the social impact of technology, engineering economics, sustainability." These are all concepts, says Rhiruvengadam Radhakrishnan, a professor of computer science and software engineering, "that are becoming more important." Indeed, this program was created in part in response to a recent declaration of the Canadian National Engineering Summit regarding the need for engineers to contribute to "a healthier, cleaner, safer, and more competitive and sustainable Canada." Furthermore, these nontechnical skills are being increasingly stressed by the Canadian Engineering Accreditation Board (McDonagh, 2011). This trend is not limited to Canada or the field of engineering (Schilling and Smith, 2010).

What universities are after, finally, is an institutional culture in which general education and the major are complementary, the courses taught are both "foundational" and "advanced," there is "synergy over duality" (Schilling and Smith, 2010, p. 34), and the two kinds of programs support each other in order to create thoughtful, deliberative graduates capable of dealing with the complex challenges of global citizenship. Wehlburg (2010) puts it this way:

> With appropriate rigor, incorporation of both areas can enhance one another. Transfer of learning may occur more easily; students may be able to bring critical-thinking or problem-solving skills gained from their general education core into their major courses. Content from the major courses may influence how a student views information in the general education courses. With integration, students might be better prepared for diverse and unexpected requirements in future careers [p. 10].

In short, the whole purpose of general education is to help students succeed in their major fields, their career choices, and their jobs. A program that is designed otherwise doesn't make sense. In addition, a well-designed general education curriculum can help major programs by creating more deliberate courses that lead to fewer failing grades and fewer students dropping classes and thus fewer wasted teaching credits; offering faculty development opportunities that enrich pedagogy in both general education and major courses; and creating interdivisional conversations that can lead to productive research collaborations. Indeed, I believe that if a general education curriculum does not have some of these benefits—or others like them—then something may be wrong.

GOALS, OBJECTIVES, LEARNING OUTCOMES, AND RELATED MATTERS

Another matter I'd like to address before heading into the main discussion has to do with academic language. Scholars familiar with contemporary thinking on course design and assessment will undoubtedly notice that my discussions of these matters doesn't get particularly technical when it comes to appropriate terminology. More specifically, I tend to blur phrases like *objectives, learning outcomes,* and *course goals.* This is a deliberate choice on my part. Partially I've been influenced by Barbara Tewksbury's excellent National Science Foundation–funded course-design workshop "The Cutting Edge." Recognizing that the correct use of these terms matters less to the people who actually teach the classes than to administrators and specialists in education, Tewksbury is explicit about using *goals* as a simple generic term to describe what an instructor hopes her students will be able to achieve on completion of a course. Having run numerous workshops at many institutions using an adaptation of Tewksbury's tutorial, I've found this approach to be appropriate and effective and have adopted it here.

I recognize that I've shortchanged a discussion of the distinctions among these terms and the ways in which institutional mission, program objectives, and course learning outcomes inform each other in a discursive manner. Once again, this was a deliberate choice on my part, made in an attempt to avoid a level of complexity that, combined with everything else in this book, seemed unnecessary. It is my hope that the other strengths of this book are enough to overcome this omission.

PART ONE

THE BIG PICTURE

CHAPTER ONE

Structuring General Education

A llow me to begin by arguing that there is no perfect general education model that is appropriate for all institutions. In fact, there are as
many models as there are institutions. Even models that look the same on
paper are likely to distinguish themselves in their implementations, the finer
details of syllabi, assignment design, day-to-day instruction, and so on.

Less obvious, but even more important, is the fact that all of these models
are different for a reason. In his seminal 1980 article "Avoiding the Potholes:
Strategies for Reforming General Education," Jerry Gaff puts it this way: "A
program for reforming general education should be designed around each
institution's character, the strengths and interests of its faculty, and the needs
of its students" (p. 50). Gaff lays out what he perceives as the forty-three
greatest mistakes an institution can fall into as it reviews and revises its
curriculum. The first "pothole" he mentions? When a university decides to
find a program to import.

DISTRIBUTION VERSUS INTEGRATION

One way to understand the variety of general education models is to place
them on a continuum, with so-called "distribution" models on one side, and
"integrative" models on the other (Figure 1.1)

Distribution
Model

Integrative
Model

Figure 1.1. Continuum of General Education Models

Although there is a need to be careful about generalizing, typically a distribution model requires students to take more or less the following courses:

- Two courses in the social sciences
- Two courses in the arts and humanities
- Two courses in mathematics
- Two courses in the natural sciences
- Two courses in a foreign language
- Two courses in physical education

Variations exist, of course. Some schools allow students to do three math and science courses, choosing two from one area and one from the other. And many institutions grant competency or Advanced Placement credit in foreign languages, mathematics, and other areas deemed appropriate.

The history of this model is long and gradual, stretching back at least as far as the nineteenth century and conceptions of what a well-rounded individual, capable of intelligent discourse, might need to study. More recently, a distributional approach to general education has often been rationalized by a university's desire to create what it refers to as "well-rounded" graduates. English majors, the thinking goes, should know enough about how science works not to be fooled by shoddy reporting in the mass media; similarly, science majors should know enough about the nature of language and its rhetorical uses to be able to distinguish truly profound literary or film art from works designed purely to manipulate emotions. Certainly these are worthy goals.

At the other end of the spectrum are models that might be described as purely integrative. Defining this term can be a little difficult, but generally it refers to a model that makes deliberate attempts to create explicit connections among courses, fields, majors, disciplines, and traditionally academic and nonacademic areas or, even better, is designed to create the opportunity for students themselves to draw those links. Thus, a curriculum might be described as integrative if it requires courses that bring together different disciplines, say, Literary Responses to Science and Technology or Mathematics and Art. Similarly, a curriculum that requires students to synthesize their seemingly disparate educational experiences in, say, a graduation portfolio or a senior capstone course might be deemed integrative. In short, I consider as integrative any curriculum that goes beyond simply requiring students to take courses from different disciplines and instead expects them, with the help of their professors, to explore the connections among these different areas.

DISTINGUISHING INTERDISCIPLINARITY AND INTEGRATION

Integrative and *interdisciplinary* are not necessarily the same thing. *Interdisciplinary* refers to programs, courses, or assignments that put together two or more distinct fields, and *integrative* more often refers to acknowledging the interdisciplinarity that already exists in a given field or topic. Therefore, *interdisciplinary*, as I'm using it here, often has an artificial quality, moving an instructor away from her discipline into other fields for which she may be less prepared. I have a degree in Victorian literature. Were I asked to teach, individually, an interdisciplinary course discussing literary exegesis and the scientific method, I might rightly argue that I'm being asked to teach something in which I have no expertise.

At the same time, I might easily teach an integrative course on science and literature in the Victorian era. Such a course would not require me to move out of my field; rather, it would ask me to use the expertise I already have regarding the period as a lens through which to discuss the science of the era. Thus, I might have students read and analyze the work of Darwin as a literary text rising from a particular social milieu or discuss the use of logic and science (or pseudoscience) in Sherlock Holmes. Similarly, I might easily teach a course discussing the pre-Raphaelite movement in literature and art or a course on sociological theory of the Victorian period and its influence on novels of the era, discussing theorists like Jeremy Bentham, Karl Marx, and Friedrich Engels, all thinkers I've already read and researched in order to better understand my field.

Similarly, asking a mathematics professor to teach, say, a course on literature and calculus might be a bit of a stretch (though many of the math professors I know are very well read). But asking a math professor to discuss how mathematics relates to, say, sports or voting methods or social theories on crime would make more sense, because these relate to things that mathematicians (depending on their specialties, of course) already do; math is already implicit within these topics. In other words, an integrative approach to curriculum is not interested in connecting things that don't come together naturally or even easily. Rather, integration encourages instructors to foreground—and students to explore—the connections that already exist between or within various fields and make the applications of our material an integral part of what we do.

Related to this, integration goes beyond interdisciplinarity in that it's often designed to connect not just one academic field to another but academic work to life beyond the classroom. A course can be integrative even if it focuses on a single field or topic as long as it explicitly asks—through lectures, discussion, and assignments—students to examine the implications of the course material on the nonacademic world and makes these explorations part of the criteria for a good grade in the class.

It's tempting, of course, to argue that every course does this. "When I teach biology," a colleague at another institution once told me, "everything I include in the syllabus is relevant to my students' lives. Every time they draw a breath—that's biology!" Such an argument can likely be made about almost anything we teach, from biology to sociology to political science to art and philosophy. There's no point, after all, in teaching something that is absolutely meaningless to students' lives.

What I'm discussing here, though, is more a matter of degree and deliberation. A course is truly integrative in nature when it does more than introduce material relevant to lived experience. It is deliberate and explicit about making those connections—and, necessarily, having students make those connections. One good example is service-learning, where students are required to apply their work in a class toward improving the lives of the larger community. A sociology course on writing grants for nonprofit organizations might have students working with programs in the community to draft and revise proposals and then writing a conclusive essay synthesizing their in-class and out-of-class experiences.

I am not saying that there is anything wrong with interdisciplinarity or that integrativeness is necessarily better. Indeed, designed carefully, interdisciplinary programs and courses can be very successful. It is not unusual, though, for faculty to feel anxiety regarding general education and the degree to which it does or does not ask them to move beyond their area of expertise. One purpose of distinguishing the two terms, then, is to alleviate these worries: curricular models or general education courses that are integrative in nature need not require faculty to teach outside their fields.

INTEGRATIVE COMPONENTS

Beyond the courses themselves, any number of structural components can make a curriculum more integrative. Requiring a common core—a class or series of classes—that all students at an institution must take regardless of major is one example. A core can create opportunities for students and instructors from a variety of disciplines to meet and discuss topics about which they are all concerned—the state of the environment, the nature of truth, and living a purposeful life, to name a few—drawing each from their own fields and learning from each other. An upper-level capstone course is one type of core component that asks students to synthesize their learning experiences in other courses they've taken, attempting to create a meaningful whole out of varied and sometimes conflicting information. Similarly, e-portfolios—an online collection of artifacts (papers, presentations, and so on) from a student's relevant work in general education and other courses—are an opportunity for students to reflect on how all of their varied educational experiences, in and out of the classroom, relate to one another and their own goals for the future.

Another structural approach to integration might include campuswide themes under which general education courses are organized. A campus might choose, for instance, strands on technology and its consequences, the role of power, or gender and race. Courses might be offered under any of these strands by any department on campus. Under the topic of technology and its consequences, for example, a biology instructor might offer a course on global warming, a sociology professor might offer a course on social networking, and a literature professor might teach a section on science fiction or constructions of future worlds. Each course would have its own syllabus, goals, and assessments, but as students move from a course in one field to another under the same strand, they are given the opportunity to see how different fields approach related topics. Thus, they come to a more meaningful understanding of both the topic and the fields. (For further discussion of this model, see Chapter Two.)

A more explicit approach to this kind of integration can be found in learning communities. In its simplest form, this method entails enrolling students in a number of courses with related topics that are offered during the same term. For example, Ferrum College in southwestern Virginia offers a learning community on Appalachian culture. In a single term, students fulfill multiple general education requirements by taking courses in sociology, environmental science, and English. Each course teaches the usual introductory terminology and methodologies crucial to its field and then makes these concepts meaningful by applying them to the culture and region in which the campus is immersed. In addition, such a structure allows students to compare how these three fields vary in their approach to the same topic—again, offering the opportunity for greater synthesis and understanding on the part of the students.

THE TREND IN GENERAL EDUCATION

The trend in general education in the United States and elsewhere seems to show a shift from purely distributional models toward models that combine distributive features with more integrative components, moving from the far left of the continuum toward the center and even slightly beyond (American Association of Colleges and Universities, 2009). A recent survey sponsored by the American Association of Colleges and Universities of 433 institutions granting a variety of degrees reports that only 15 percent of responding institutions used models that had purely distributional attributes. Similarly,

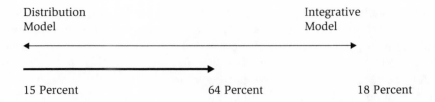

Figure 1.2. Recent Trends in American General Education

18 percent had models that consisted only of what the survey termed "other components"—integrative features such as required thematic courses, core courses, and learning communities. Fully 64 percent of the institutions reported having models that combined distributional components with these "other" integrative features (American Association of Colleges and Universities, 2009; see Figure 1.2).

The reasons for this shift away from distributional models vary by university, state, and country—and different scholars point to different sociological and educational trends in an attempt to explain this seismic development in tertiary education. Gaston (2010a), for instance, lists seven "drivers of change." Nevertheless, I'd like to point to four sometimes intertwining causes: the complexity of students' lives, the rapid growth of knowledge in our fields, the changing nature of the workplace, and the challenges of citizenship in today's world.

Our Students' Lives

It's astounding to think about how fragmented our students' lives can be. Every semester they take multiple courses that cover multiple chapters from multiple books on multiple topics in multiple fields; they write multiple papers, give multiple oral presentations, and take multiple exams; they do these things in major courses, minor courses, elective courses, and those pesky general education courses; they have practicum, labs, internships, work-study, off-campus jobs—and sometimes all of the above. Then they have their dorm lives, their social lives (often two very different things), their spiritual lives, service-learning projects, and other work in the community. As opposed to their professors, who grew up at a time when it was unusual to communicate with their parents more than once a week, for today's students, cell phones, Facebook, texting, and Skype ensure that their home lives—their families, their high school friends—are just as present and demanding as their school lives. They face a plethora of information, a virtual blizzard of factoids that they encounter hourly from blogs, Twitter, and the traditional media. Given all of this, it's astounding that any students are capable of forming a cohesive thought.

One reason so many general education programs are becoming increasingly integrative is that this approach seeks to create more deliberate—and deliberative—moments when students can make sense of the often disparate information they're receiving and the often contradictory experiences they are having. Put another way, an integrative approach to general education creates synthesizing opportunities. I've already mentioned some of the ways a curriculum might do this through capstone courses, e-portfolios, or learning communities. Similarly, carefully designed courses might foreground the interplay among seemingly different topics.

A mathematician might create a course exploring the ways in which mathematics plays itself out in various forms of classical music, thereby deliberately breaking down assumptions about the seeming disconnect between these two fields. A statistician might create an assignment asking students to apply statistical methods to social justice—thus connecting math to social science, community service, and students' own values system.

Or an instructor might assign a paper requiring students from a variety of fields to deliberate on how the course content relates to their own field. For instance, in a recent nonmajor class on the social functions of poetry, students were asked to write an essay to the director of their major programs explaining why the study of poetry would be useful to undergraduates in that field. The results were telling: a premed student wrote that poetry could increase a doctor's empathy for her patients; a criminal justice major (and a veteran of the Iraq war) wrote about how studying literature can help us better understand ourselves, crucial for a police officer or lawyer facing a potentially soul-breaking situation.

Now consider a more difficult example. What would happen in a general education sociology course if an English major were given the assignment of analyzing why someone who studies literature might benefit from an understanding of the various forces that drive social interaction? What might an art major required to analyze the relation of chemistry to her field explore about the mixing of paints, the restoration of old works, an understanding of impressionism? What might a prelaw student come to understand about how an environmental science course might be relevant as he chooses a career path?

What a student finally writes in a particular paper (or oral presentation or exam question) about a particular course, though, pales in comparison to the cognitive skill she will develop as she attempts to apply information learned in one setting to another, as she tries to draw connections where, sixteen weeks earlier, she saw none. Courses and assignments of this sort offer students the opportunity to put things together, make a meaningful whole, look at contradictions and work them out, weigh options, and make choices that are thoughtful and enriching rather than hasty and inconsequential. This skill, practiced over and over again over the course of students' four or more years at university, will allow them to move forward in a world flooded with information and connections and disconnections and respond in a productive manner.

The Exponential Growth of Knowledge in Our Fields

In nearly every field, knowledge is growing quantitatively and qualitatively. Forty years ago, for example, literature studies in the United States were concerned largely with Western—and, generally, white male—texts, giving the occasional nod to non-Western works only in the context of their influence on European and American writers.

Since the 1980s, however, there has been an explosion of interest in non-Western and multiethnic, diasporic literatures. The canon, as a result, has grown. Where previously it was considered enough that an English major know Chaucer, Shakespeare, Dickens, Eliot, and so on, now departments must make careful decisions about how these authors should or should not be balanced by explorations of Toni Morrison, Amy Tan, Louise Erdrich, and others.

The reading of literature has also changed qualitatively. Where once literary theory was considered marginal—or even optional—for undergraduate studies, now most B.A. programs require at least one or two courses that are less interested in reading primary texts than in exploring the nature of that reading: how the various critical lenses readers apply to a text can change their understanding of it. Put another way, conceptions of what is necessary to be an effective English major have changed in a three-dimensional manner—spreading and broadening, but also spiraling upward. The very nature of the field has changed.

The discipline of English is by no means alone. As Julie Thompson Klein (2010) has pointed out, in the past few decades, many majors have demonstrated a "greater porosity of boundaries" (p. 156). In the sciences, for instance, the once fairly clear lines among physics, chemistry, and biology have become increasingly blurred. Whereas chemists once generally thought of themselves as specializing in one of several specialties (organic, inorganic, physical, and so on), now they may be part of a larger interdisciplinary team focused on a single problem. Thus, a chemist interested in drug discovery and development may find herself working closely with biochemists, synthetic organic chemists, computer scientists, and molecular biologists. Similarly, a physicist might go into medical physics, biological physics, materials physics, and so on. Meanwhile, string theory brings with it a kind of qualitative change, reshaping not just what we know but how we think about what we know.

Consider the study of psychology, where advances in technology have expanded our understanding of the mind. Using functional magnetic imaging, CAT scans, brain surgery, and new drugs, psychologists are adding new information about parts of the brain we've long known about and discovering areas we hadn't even realized were there. And here too there's a qualitative change: the discipline becomes more integrative, developing fields that combine different areas, for instance, cross-cultural psychology or neuropsychology and evolutionary psychology. In these fields — and indeed, in most other fields — a textbook is out of date the minute it hits our desk — never mind four years down the road when students enter the workplace.

We're living at a time when we cannot possibly, in a four- or even five-year curriculum, teach students everything they need to know in our fields — even if we, as I've seen one institution do, create majors that take up 70 percent of a student's credit hours. Certainly we need to give students as much information as we can — or as much as their developing brains can take, which is not necessarily the same thing. In the end, though, we also need to prepare them to encounter new and unexpected information, evaluate the quality of that information, and find ways to reconcile that information with what they already know.

Here again an integrative approach to general education can be valuable, particularly when it is incorporated into a distributive model. As students move from one field to another in a distributional curriculum, they are constantly encountering new information, new ways of looking at the world, and new ways of thinking about and solving problems. By taking an integrative approach to these encounters, universities and individual instructors provide opportunities for students to explore in deliberate ways the connections and disconnections between new ideas and ideas and knowledge they they've already incorporated into their worldview.

This deliberateness is essential; it is not enough to simply be exposed to information. Exposure, particularly to information that is outside a student's field with no obvious connection to his or her long-term goals, will lead to short-term engagement at best: learn the material, take the test, get the grade, and move on to the next course.

In contrast, structuring metacognitive moments in the design of the course, the design of the assignments, or through some added feature such as e-portfolios gives students the opportunity to think about what's going on and consider how the skills and the ways of thinking in one class might be applied to another, seemingly entirely different, class. In this way, they begin to learn how to respond in effective ways when faced with new information, new challenges, new ways of thinking: Where have they seen problems like this before? What strategies did they use to help solve those problems? To what degree might those strategies work here? To what degree need they be changed to meet this new situation? In this way, an effective integrative approach prepares students for the changing nature of knowledge, even in their own fields.

The Changing Nature of the Workplace

A third point that may explain the increasing use of integrative approaches to general education relates to the day-to-day realities of the workplace. One of the beauties of academia—for students, at least—is that they always know where they are. On the first day of class, their professors hand out syllabi labeled, "Political Science 101," "English 401," "STAT 1210," or "BIOL 220." There's a level of reassurance in this. It's nice to be able to say, "Now I'm going to study chemistry," or "Today I have classes in art, sociology, and history," or, "Tomorrow I have a project due in communications."

Unfortunately, that's not how most jobs work. An architect, for example, might begin the morning doing design, then go to a work site to talk to the contractor, next meet with a potential client to discuss building a new synagogue, and end the day at a city council meeting debating the subtleties of zoning permits. Although we can recognize the various fields implicit in these actions (engineering, management, sociology, religion, history, and politics), in the reality outside academia, these tasks blur together. Is the discussion of the new synagogue engineering, religion, politics, history, or sociology? Is the town council meeting more about business, sociology, politics, or management?

In the end, of course, the designation doesn't matter. Work is work, and the architect—like the guidance counselor, the pharmacist, the restaurant owner, the chief financial officer—must deal with each challenge the best she can.

Complicating all of this is the fact that the work world is changing rapidly. In *Two-Way Mirrors: Cross-Cultural Studies in Glocalization (2007)*, Eugene Eoyang makes the argument that the very nature of work has shifted dramatically. Glossing through three hundred years of modern history, Eoyang asserts that the expectations of employers with regard to their employees have evolved from labor (preindustry), to skills (during the Industrial Revolution), to knowledge (from the 1940s to the 1980s), to insight (today).

For our purposes, the most intriguing shift here is between knowledge and insight, with *knowledge* often used to refer solely to content and *insight* more about process. *Knowledge*, as I'm using it here, is quantitative: Do you have the information, yes or no? Do you have the right information, yes or no? Insight is qualitative—not just, "Do you know X and Y?" but, "When X and Y fail, what ideas, thoughts, or cognitive paradigms do you have that will allow you to respond to this new, unanticipated problem?" Insight of course requires knowledge; students in any field need to know the concepts of that field. But insight is also able to move one beyond the known and the familiar into the unanticipated and unfamiliar.

Here's another way to think about it. Edmond Ko, an engineering professor formerly at Carnegie Mellon University and now at the Hong Kong University of Science and Technology, speaks eloquently of "wicked problems": challenges in engineering and other fields where the boundaries of the problem shift rapidly because of information that is incomplete, contradictory, or continually changing. Ko, who is experienced in curricular design and an advocate for integrative learning, makes the point that engineers faced with wicked problems must have "wicked competencies"—in other words, the ability to adapt to a rapidly shifting landscape.

Although it's true that many of us (maybe even all of us) in the academy thrive by focusing our energy on narrowly defined topics—indeed, sometimes the narrower, the better—that's rarely the world for which we're preparing our students. Like engineers, accountants also face wicked problems, with laws shifting from year to year and even quarter to quarter. So too city managers must take into account changing budgets, directors of information technology constantly face new bugs and new technologies, and editors daily learn whole new fields in order to provide effective feedback to authors.

In short, employers are looking for graduates who demonstrate wicked competencies, as evidenced by a recent survey of businesses and other organizations that employ college graduates (American Association of Colleges and Universities, 2009):

- Ninety-one percent of the employers surveyed said that their employees were being asked to "use a broader set of skills than in the past."
- Eighty-eight percent of those surveyed said that "the challenges employees face within our company today are more complex than they were in the past."

Our students' work will require them to stretch daily, if not hourly, outside their undergraduate fields. Their work worlds will present them with problems that don't look like those they read about in the textbooks we assigned them, the problems they faced their first week on the job, or even the problems they struggled with at the beginning of the calendar year.

Not surprisingly, there is evidence that employers want graduates who demonstrate the flexibility of mind necessary to respond to the wicked problems of the workplace. In the same American Association of Colleges and Universities (2009) survey, employers were presented with seventeen possible university-wide learning outcomes and asked to state which ones they felt colleges should place more emphasis on. Three of the top seven items they chose involved the sorts of adaptive skills supported by an integrative approach to general education:

- Developing critical thinking and analytical reasoning skills (item 2, with an 81 percent support rate)
- The ability to analyze and solve complex problems (item 4, with a 75 percent support rate)
- The ability to innovate and be creative (item 7, with a 70 percent support rate)

Indeed, one could argue that the other four items at the top of this list—effective communication skills, the ability to apply knowledge in real-world situations, the ability to make ethical decisions, and teamwork skills (American Association of Colleges and Universities, 2009) — also require the flexibility to respond to constantly shifting demands, be they rhetorical, moral, institutional, or otherwise.

The evolution of integrative learning occurred in response to the needs of this constantly changing workplace. An integrative approach asks students to be deliberative about their explorations of various fields — not just to experience these courses, but to think about how they fit into their own lives, their professional goals, their worldviews. For instance, as a student participating in a learning community in global climate change exits a biology lab on Great Plains ecosystems and ventures forth into her linked course on the politics of environmentalism, she should be asked to think about how the day's reading on polling methods can affect public policy on fertilizer runoff. Even better, the instructors of one or both of these courses might assign a final paper requiring students to detail the ways in which an ecosystem discussed in the biology class has been affected by procedural policies in the state capital.

Similarly, an institution might implement an e-portfolio policy that requires each student to provide a scholarly artifact — for example, an essay, project, or oral presentation — from each course of his or her term, then write a brief essay that explains the connections and disconnects he or she perceives among those fields. Thus, a student might find himself thinking about how his major course in twentieth-century physics relates to his required distribution course in romantic poetry — and writing an eloquent argument about string theory and Coleridge's "The Eolian Harp." That such an exercise might strengthen the learning in both courses is worth noting. As Peggy Maki (2010) points out, "Self-reflection reinforces learning by engaging learners in focused thinking about their understanding and misunderstanding" (p. 48). In other words, the student learns the material in the course, under the guidance of the instructor, in a setting that is bounded on one side by the beginning of the term and on the other by the final exam. And then the student learns the material again, on his or her own, this time outside the traditional classroom, as he attempts to make connections that have nothing to do with exams, grades, or letters of recommendation, and everything to do with making sense out of two seemingly disparate topics, and between these topics and one's own life goals.

The Challenges of Citizenship in Today's World

What all of this — the explosion of media, the growth of knowledge, the challenges of globalism — adds up to is a world where emerging graduates are overwhelmed with information — factoids, sound bites, polemics, and data. Some of it is real and accurate and some of it blatantly false, but all of it needs to be sifted and sorted, evaluated for accuracy, relevance, and efficacy. Paul Gaston (2010a) states it in this way:

> Never before has there been so great a need for learned and adaptable citizens capable of taking apart and understanding complex problems, of identifying reliability and authority among the many sources of information, of appreciating the quantitative realities that may lie beneath the surface, of thinking creatively about solutions, of communicating *to* others the emerging results of their work, and of working *with* others to bring solutions to practice [p. 10].

Such a world requires knowledge drawn from a variety of fields. When an oil rig explodes in the Gulf of Mexico, citizens should be able to accurately understand the consequences, short term and long term, of the disaster (biology, chemistry), should not be entirely reliant on the media for discerning responsibility (politics, journalism, textual exegesis) and degrees of culpability (business, government policy, ethics), and should be able to respond to the situation in an informed, deliberative, and productive way.

Were university education a ten-year endeavor allowing over a thousand credit hours, delivering the content that would create such a citizen possible might be feasible. But that is not the case. Students who do remain in academia for a decade generally do so in order to become highly focused professionals versed in a small corner of a narrow field. The rest grab what they can in a four- or five-year stint. We can give them a distribution of knowledge, but we can't possibly cover everything they need to know to react thoughtfully to today's increasingly globalized, technological, polarized world. In other words, citizenship in today's world requires graduates to have the intellectual and cognitive skills that allow them to respond to new information (whether it was "covered" in a course or not) by calling on past experiences, some similar, some not; seeking out appropriate background information; evaluating data carefully and thoughtfully; and being capable of synthesizing disparate ideas in order to respond accordingly. Even more, citizenship today requires graduates who can anticipate these problems and effectively combine business acumen with ethics and political efficacy with environmental sensitivity. In short, citizenship today needs an integrative approach to university education that goes beyond exposure and toward synthesis, deliberation, and application.

CONCLUSION

As students move from field to field and are asked to intellectualize that movement, several things happen:

- They have the chance to get used to constantly facing new problems, new challenges, new ways of thinking, new ways of approaching the world.

- They are provided the opportunity to see patterns that might not at first be obvious to them—the ways in which, for instance, a scientific insistence on objectivity is also essential for literary exegesis or how the challenges of writing a computer program relate to the efficiency of language in poetry.

- They are given the chance to experiment with transferring and adapting problem-solving strategies—to see, for instance, how the methods they learned in psychology last semester can be adapted to the new and different challenges of an art history course.

In the end, an integrative approach to general education seeks to create an academic world that mimics more closely the wicked problems of today's work world. And more to the point, integrative general education attempts to be deliberate about providing graduates with the wicked competencies they will need to be productive citizens in that world.

CHAPTER TWO

Some Examples of Integrative Curricular Models

The kind of structure an institution designs and where it lands along the continuum from distribution to integration will be influenced by any number of things. Some colleges and universities, for instance, may quickly realize that they already have a great number of integrative programs and a faculty that is comfortable with cross-disciplinary collaborations; they may place themselves somewhere on the far right of this scale. Other institutions may balk at the perceived logistical difficulties of a high level of integration and place themselves further to the left. Nevertheless, every institution should recognize that where it places itself on this continuum will have consequences in two important areas.

The first of these is the degree of integration the students will need to perform on their own. At the simplest level, a purely distributional model on the far left of the continuum leaves it up to students to think about how biology and history, political science and statistics, or music history and psychology relate to one another. At the other end is a model that does not do all the work for the students but is deliberate about providing opportunities for synthesis and integration and coaches that process carefully.

This may sound like an unabashed endorsement for a more integrative approach, as does this comment by Jonathan Smith, a former dean of the college at the University of Chicago, who once declared a single "iron law": "Students shall not be expected to integrate anything the faculty can't or won't" (quoted in Gaff, 1980, p. 55). And certainly there's some wisdom to such an approach: after all, if the faculty, with their advanced degrees and years of worldly experience and complex ways of thinking, are not deliberate about creating structures that allow integration, then the chances that any but the best of a body of young and inexperienced students will achieve high levels of cognitive synthesis are unlikely. At the same time, of course, a professor can't do a student's learning for her. If a developing scholar is to acquire the competencies necessary for the changing workplace, she is going to have to take the lead in achieving that learning.

The point here is that in the process of developing a new curricular model, faculty should think carefully about the students at their institution, their goals for these students, and the needs of their students as they decide where along the continuum the institution's model should be placed. To develop a program that won't work for the students and won't create an environment that allows them to do their best work is a waste of time.

The second important area is the frequency and quality of interdivisional conversations among the faculty. Here again the point is fairly simple: a purely distributional model in which faculty concentrate on teaching courses that introduce their fields and make very few gestures toward integration will require only minimal conversations between departments and divisions. Certainly there will be some discussion of standards and criteria, and these conversations will be valuable, but they will likely occur only occasionally, most often early in the implementation process.

Even a moderately integrated model, where faculty from across the divisions are teaching an interdisciplinary core course or a series of linked courses, will require greater coordination and a higher frequency of interdepartmental and interdivisional conversation. Instructors will need to meet not just at the beginning of the program or the beginning of the academic year, but likely throughout the term as they seek to ensure that the content they're providing and the assignments they are creating are in keeping with the work of their colleagues.

The benefits of these kinds of continuing interdisciplinary conversations can extend well beyond day-to-day logistics. Linguists have known for years that small talk is often anything but inconsequential. As we chat with one another about the weather or nagging health issues, we're developing a shared discourse and common understandings that make our future interactions more efficient and productive. Similarly, whenever faculty from different departments come together to discuss reading lists and assignment design and assessment, they often end up discussing the things that really drive their work: their students, their own research, how to make the classroom more effective. These conversations have a practical value beyond the task at hand: they disperse effective practices across campus, create a network of support, build a sense of community, and even, perhaps, improve job quality and quality of life. And as Gaff and Ratcliff (1997) point out, all of this also works for the benefit of the students.

THREE CURRICULAR MODELS

An institution that is developing a new curricular model should think carefully about the impact a particular type of program will have on the institution as a whole. What interactions might a particular structure create? To what extent might these be valuable to the forward progress of the university?

The three curricular models that follow show varying approaches to integration. They are included here for illustrative purposes only, and should by no means be read as prescriptive. Indeed, it's important to remember Gaff's assertion that the biggest mistake any college or university can make is to adopt from another school a model that doesn't fit its own institutional culture. Nonetheless, these models may be helpful as an illustration of integrative concepts put into practice and a means of beginning discussions about creating effective integrative models of general education.

The Strands Model

The strands model is a fairly straightforward structure wherein courses from the various disciplines are designed around a number of relevant themes or topical strands. One of its strengths is that it allows both disciplinary expertise and interdisciplinary conversations.

Essentially the model operates on a two-dimensional grid—for example:

	Strand A	Strand B	Strand C
Social sciences			
Mathematics and the natural sciences			
Arts and humanities			

On the left-hand side are the disciplinary perspectives as they've been constructed in the late twentieth- and early twenty-first centuries: the social sciences, mathematics and the natural sciences, and the arts and humanities. Students are required to take a designated number of courses within each of the disciplinary groupings—for example, two courses from fields in the social sciences, two from fields in the arts and humanities, and so on.

So far this is a fairly traditional distributional model. It becomes more integrative when each of the course offerings from each of the disciplines is grouped into a particular, broadly defined theme, or intellectual strand, that is shared campuswide. What exactly these strands are will, of course, be determined by the institution. As an example, let's say that University A has chosen three themes:

	The Consequences of Science and Technology	America and Its Relationship with the World	What It Means to Be Human
Social sciences			
Mathematics and the natural sciences			
Arts and humanities			

An institution taking this approach would need to define the parameters of each strand. Let's say that courses in "The Consequences of Science and Technology" strand must use the methodology of the instructor's field to address the actual, perceived, or imagined impact of technological and scientific advances; courses appropriate for the "America and Its Relationship with the World" strand must address the United States, a place or places outside the United States, and the interaction between the two in today's globalized and complicated world; and approved classes for the "What It Means to Be Human" strand would look at the ways in which a particular field explores the scientific, sociological, psychological, and emotional definitions, limitations, and consequences of the human condition.

Within each of these areas, departments can offer courses that address that strand's theme from their disciplinary perspective. Thus, under "The Consequences of Science and Technology," a student might find (among others) the following offerings:

	The Consequences of Science and Technology	America and Its Relationship with the World	What It Means to Be Human
Social sciences	The Changing Face of Personal Interaction (Sociology) How Your iPod Is Changing Your Brain (Psychology)		
Mathematics and the natural sciences	Cyberspying (Information Technology)		

	The Consequences of Science and Technology	America and Its Relationship with the World	What It Means to Be Human
	Ethics and the Human Genome (Biology) Vanishing Species (Biology)		
Arts and humanities	Romanticism and the Industrial Revolution (English) Composition and Computers (Music)		

Under "America and Its Relationship with the World," students might discover courses that address both the United States and the rest of the world, making explicit concepts of citizenship in an increasingly globalized world. Here are some possible offerings:

For the social sciences

- Women in Leadership Roles (Political Science)
- Comparative Psychology (Psychology)

For mathematics and the natural sciences

- Space and Space Technology (Physics)
- The Statistics of Gun Control (Mathematics)
- The Changing Pacific (Environmental Science)

For arts and humanities

- The African Diaspora (Literature)
- Asia and Modernism (Art History)

The "What It Means to Be Human" strand could include a wide variety of courses from any number of fields:

For the social sciences

- Does Personality Exist? (Psychology)

For mathematics and the natural sciences

- The Human Genome (Biology)

For arts and humanities

- What Is the Mind? (Philosophy)
- Free Will and Other Myths (Philosophy)

Indeed, a strand of this sort might even contain similarly titled courses offered by very different fields as part of its offerings:

For the social sciences

- Understanding Violence (Sociology)

For mathematics and the natural sciences

- Understanding Violence (Statistics)

For arts and humanities

- Understanding Violence (Drama)

In this last example, each field would approach the topic of violence from its particular disciplinary perspective. Students who took all three courses—or were required to take all three courses—would then have the opportunity to come to a better understanding of violence (or gender, or game theory, or poverty) from three very different methodologies. With an approach like this, no coordination would be necessary among the professors, and no professor would be required to step outside his or her area of expertise, but students would nonetheless have an integrative opportunity. Of course, if the institution and the professors felt comfortable with it, some degree—even a very large degree—of collaboration among the three courses would be possible, creating an even richer learning experience for students.

Regardless, recognizing that the courses we've been discussing thus far are only a sampling of the types of offerings that might be available under the strands the institution has chosen, the curriculum as a whole might end up looking something like this:

	The Consequences of Science and Technology	America and Its Relationship with the World	What It Means to Be Human
Social sciences	The Changing Face of Personal Interaction (Sociology)	Women in Leadership Roles (Political Science)	Does Personality Exist? (Psychology)
	How Your iPod Is Changing Your Brain (Psychology)	Comparative Psychology (Psychology)	Understanding Violence (Sociology)

	The Consequences of Science and Technology	America and Its Relationship with the World	What It Means to Be Human
Mathematics and the natural sciences	Cyberspying (Information Technology)	Space and Space Technology (Physics)	The Human Genome (Biology)
	Ethics and the Human Genome (Biology)	The Statistics of Gun Control (Mathematics)	Understanding Violence (Statistics)
	Vanishing Species (Biology)	The Changing Pacific (Environmental Science)	
Arts and humanities	Romanticism and the Industrial Revolution (English)	The African Diaspora (Literature)	What Is the Mind?
	Composition and Computers (Music)	Asia and Modernism (Art History)	Free Will and Other Myths (Philosophy)
			Understanding Violence (Drama)

Specific offerings would be determined by the interests and specializations of the faculty in a given department. And the strands chosen should match the interests, abilities, and culture of the institution. Indeed, strands might even be chosen to emphasize the geographical location of the school, the unique history of the region, or the philosophical or religious leanings of the institution.

In addition to meeting distributional obligations across the disciplines, students in the strand model might be required to take a specified number of courses (usually one or two) in each strand. Because they would likely take six or seven courses across the three strands, students would see at least a couple of disciplinary approaches to the broader themes. In this way, an institution could ensure that not only do students explore a number of fields, they also explore some of the major issues that drive the work of the university—and work beyond the university—from a multiplicity of perspectives.

Alternatively, students might be asked to fulfill all of their distributional requirements within a single strand. Although such an approach might limit the kinds of questions students might explore, it does have the advantage of focusing students' explorations of disciplinary perspectives. Looking at the issue of, say, technology from six different perspectives (two from each division) allows a greater complexity to one's understanding of how different fields approach a subject. Some institutions might prefer such an approach over one that would spread the same six courses over three different questions, thereby allowing only dual perspectives on each matter. The choice comes down to what the university values.

While such a model obviously allows integration for students—looking at a single question from multiple disciplinary viewpoints—it also creates more campuswide conversations even beyond the student body. A faculty choosing this approach would need to coordinate both horizontally and vertically across the institution. Within a division—say, the sciences—there would need to be a conversation among the mathematicians, the chemists, the biologists, the physicists, and others to determine the shared goals across the three strands. The common denominators would then ensure that students taking chemistry in strand A were understanding scientific methods as rigorously and effectively as those taking biology in strand C.

Similarly, there would have to be a conversation within each vertical strand to coordinate exactly what it means for a course to be a part of that theme. What, for example, makes a course appropriate for the "What It Means to Be Human" strand, as opposed to the "Consequences of Science and Technology" strand? And would there be any common academic outcomes of each strand? Would a student in a technology strand need to be able to show competency in basic information technology skills? What would students who participated in a global strand need to be able to do or say or show to demonstrate that they'd achieved the institution's goals relative to that strand?

In short, this model necessitates both intra- and interdivisional conversations among faculty. Without these conversations, the kinds of integration we'd be asking students to perform would be virtually impossible. And while some faculty may be inclined to roll their eyes at the thought of having to take time to conduct all of these conversations within their disciplines and with brethren in more distant fields, the fact is that conversations like this allow institutions to stay on track, ensuring a shared vision of education from one end of campus to another. Furthermore, such an approach can help to assimilate new faculty into the university, a step that can contribute to avoiding the need for a full-fledged curricular revision every ten years as faculty come and go, institutional memory fades, and the curriculum and individual courses drift from their initial intent.

The Core-Distributional Model

A core-distributional model combines distributional requirements with core courses—that is, courses that are required of all students regardless of their major, and often (though not always) taught by faculty from across campus.

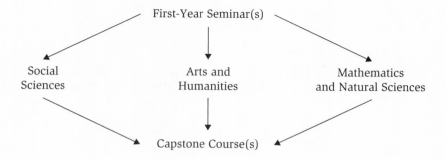

Figure 2.1. A Core-Distributional Model

Figure 2.1 is a model developed in the early stages of a curricular revision by a university in Asia. In this model, students begin in a common course, the first-year seminar (FYS); fulfill a number of distribution requirements; and finish their studies in a common course. The idea is that the FYS prepares students for their distribution courses, providing them some of the skills necessary for success, and the capstone course provides students with a synthetic experience, allowing them to draw everything together. Paradoxically, an institution might improve the motivation of students in their sophomore and junior years by designing the model in such a way that the knowledge they gained from the distribution classes was essential for success at the capstone level.

Any number of variables exist with a model like this. Institutions might, for instance, place the capstone in the major rather than in the general education program. (Whether this approach is better is debatable, but regardless of where the capstone is placed, care should be taken to ensure that it touches on both the major and general education, because both will be essential to success in the workplace.) Institutions developing a model along these lines will also need to explore how integrated the distributional components in the middle of the curriculum should be. As Ann Ferren (2010) notes, "Critics of the undergraduate experience find in programs evidence of a good start and a strong finish but a 'muddle in the middle.' Intentionally designed programs address this concern by framing what should happen not just in the first year but also in the second, third, and fourth years. Education is, as it should be, cumulative, with opportunities for reinforcement at many stages" (p. 28).

Some institutions might also include arrows connecting the three types of distribution courses in Figure 2.1, indicating that these classes should also be integrative in nature, not simply teaching their ideas and methodologies in isolation from other learning (Figure 2.2).

Again, one of the major issues facing a school that's creating a new curriculum is the degree to which the integrative work of the students is supported by the design of the curriculum. After all, asking students to make connections

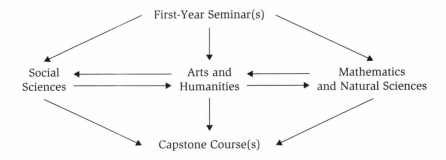

Figure 2.2. A Fully Integrated Core-Distributional Model

between standard Biology 101 and Literary Analysis 101 is very different from asking them to synthesize the content of a course entitled "Appalachian Ecosystems" and "Ecocriticism and Romantic Literature." In the first example, no gesture is made on the part of the instructors toward moving the ideas of the course beyond the walls of the classroom. By contrast, in the other example, course content is being applied to actual practical situations (Appalachia's forests) and being used to make connections between different fields of study (English and environmentalism).

Questions must also be answered about the nature of the first-year seminar (or seminars). Will this be an Introduction to College course that covers the nuts-and-bolts survival skills a student will need not to flunk out after a single term? Or will this be a Great Questions course that introduces students to high intellectual expectations and a challenging reading load? Or somewhere in between? Are these seminars smaller than typical courses? Are they taught by faculty from across campus or by a few departments? Will every first-year seminar have the same syllabus, or will they vary? Will they be writing intensive, requiring not just the assigning of writing but the application of writing-specific pedagogies, such as paper conferences and peer-response sessions?

Implicit within this discussion is the fact that the core-distributive model and the strands model are by no means exclusive. Indeed, Roanoke College in Salem, Virginia, employs a model that combines the two. It begins with a pair of first-year seminars (one that is writing intensive and theme based, the other of which focuses on ethics and oral communication); then it requires that students take seven distribution courses over the three disciplines from a number of offered strands: "The Natural World," "The West," and "Globalization." Finally, students take a junior-level capstone course that is part of the Intellectual Inquiries general education program.

The Core-Only Model

Perhaps a more radical approach is the one adopted more than forty years ago by St. Joseph's College in Rensselaer, Indiana. This model contains ten courses that all students take, regardless of their major, and it is taught broadly by faculty from across campus:

Term 1	Term 2
The Contemporary Situation	The Modern World
The Roots of Civilization	Christian Impact on Western Civilization
Humanity in the Universe I	Humanity in the Universe II
Intercultural Studies I	Intercultural Studies II

Capstone I:	Capstone II:
Toward a Christian Humanism I	Toward a Christian Humanism Seminars

What makes this model distinctive is that it consists of only a core: every student on campus, no matter what his or her major, takes all of these courses. The courses themselves are fairly interdisciplinary. During one recent term, the faculty teaching The Modern World came from departments as varied as art, mathematics, psychology, and business management. Even courses with a more disciplinary content—Humanity in the Universe, for instance, essentially a science class—are taught by faculty drawn from a range of fields, including biology, psychology, chemistry, mathematics, and education. The faculty teaching a particular offering of a course get together every semester to plan exactly what will occur during the term.

The logistics of this particular core, as St. Joseph's has developed it, involves shared lectures followed by smaller classes (sixteen to eighteen students) with a particular instructor. During these smaller sessions, students discuss their readings and the lecture and writing assignments, and they take quizzes and tests.

That many of these courses are religious in nature is, for our purposes, beside the point—or, perhaps, it is entirely the point. An actively Catholic college, St. Joseph's has decided to make Christian humanism the overarching theme of its core. Other institutions might choose social justice, ethics, globalism, or other themes that reflect the challenges of productive and active participation in today's world. In the end, what the core-only model offers is a curricular structure that foregrounds the interconnections among different fields, different methodologies, and different ways of looking at the world. That an institution might find an approach to achieving this goal that highlights its unique history and culture is a bonus.

St. Joseph's revises the core on a fairly regular basis in order to ensure relevance. In a recent iteration, Intercultural Studies I focused on China, while Intercultural Studies II focused on Latin America. At other times, these courses have looked at Africa or Asia more broadly. In addition to keeping the core current, this approach ensures constant communication among faculty from across campus. This is important in that it helps to create a community of shared values and practices, brings new faculty into important discussions, and helps to avoid curricular drift.

SOME ADDITIONAL MODELS

The following models, admittedly chosen rather arbitrarily, provide a greater sense of the myriad possible ways a school can address the challenge of preparing students for a rapidly changing world. Faculty interested in knowing more about these models can go to the Web sites I've provided or contact university administrators for further information.

Wagner College, Staten Island, New York

When Wagner revised its curriculum, it made a point of highlighting its location in New York City, emphasizing service-learning and other components that make use of the metropolitan area. The Wagner Plan requires that students

- Participate in at least three learning communities: one their first year, one their senior year in the major, and one somewhere in between.

- Participate in extensive experiential learning activities linked to their first-year and senior-year learning communities.

- Complete at least ten units with disciplinary perspectives: three each in the humanities and social sciences and two each in the natural sciences (including a lab) and the arts. These courses overlay with the learning communities and other components of the Wagner Plan.

- Take courses in or demonstrate competencies in writing, mathematics, oral communication, and computers.

The first-year learning communities at Wagner consist of three courses linked by a common theme and a shared set of students; overlapping assignments, common readings, and "joint problems"; and a smaller reflective tutorial that emphasizes writing and in which the instructor is also the students' academic advisor.

The senior-year learning communities at Wagner are in the majors, so each is slightly different. Nevertheless, each generally consists of a capstone course, a reflective tutorial, and some kind of experiential project and is designed to "sum up the Wagner student's undergraduate education."

For more information, go to www.wagner.edu/wagner_plan/.

Portland State University, Portland, Oregon

Portland State's program consists of four carefully designed levels.

Freshman Inquiry. This is a year-long, theme-based course with these features:

- It's taught by multiple instructors from various disciplines who work as a team.

- Each course is designed to look at a particular topic from different perspectives.

- There are smaller mentor sections facilitated by an upper-level student.

- Each mentor section includes student-led discussions based on homework assignments.

- The overriding theme for this course is the concept of exploration.

Sophomore Inquiry and Clusters. This pair of components foregrounds the ways in which general education courses are linked to learning throughout the university. More specifically, this portion of the program works as follows.

Students are required to take three Sophomore Inquiry (SINQ) courses that are specifically designed for the general education program.

Once students have completed all three of their SINQ courses, they must choose one of the SINQ courses that particularly appealed to them and then take three preapproved cluster courses in this area. These courses, drawn from offerings that already exist as part of other programs from across campus, offer students a means of exploring the ways in which the SINQ topic is played out in a variety of fields. For instance, a student might choose to take as his or her SINQ courses Environmental Sustainability, American Studies, and Science in the Liberal Arts. If this student especially enjoyed Environmental Sustainability, he could then choose to take any three from a list of over thirty courses from different programs, including

- Fundamentals of Environmental Design
- Severe Weather
- International Green Building and Development
- Environmental Ethics
- Ecology and the Implication of Management
- Population Trends and Policy
- Modeling Socio-Ecological Systems
- Urban Planning: Environmental Issues

As with the FYI courses, all SINQ courses also have upperclass students as peer mentors who work closely with enrollees. All cluster-approved courses have a "U" designation (for example, Urban Planning: Environmental Issues is USP 313U). The various offerings clustered with a particular SINQ course are available online, and students understand that not all courses are available all semesters.

Senior Capstones. Portland State's senior capstone courses are designed to be "the culmination of the University Studies program." They

- Build "cooperative learning communities" by bringing together students from a variety of majors.
- Ask students to "bring together the knowledge, skills, and interest developed to this point through all aspects of their education."
- Make explicit the connection between integrative liberal education and productive citizenship by directing students out into the larger community to "find solutions for issues that are important" to "literate and engaged citizens."

For more information, go to www.pdx.edu/unst/unst-introduction.

Worcester Polytechnic Institute, Worcester, Massachusetts

Worcester Polytechnic Institute (WPI) focuses largely on the fields of engineering, science, and management, although it has graduate students in the humanities as well. Here again there's an emphasis on citizenship. Part of the goal of WPI is to "convey the latest science and engineering knowledge in ways that would be most useful to the society from which its students came." The undergraduate program consists of several distinct but related components.

The First-Year Experience. All first-year students are assigned to "insight teams" consisting of faculty advisers, resident advisors, and student leaders referred to as "community advisors." These teams plan activities, both academic and otherwise, relating to the challenges of making a successful transition to university life.

Great Problems Seminars, two-term courses that extend over fourteen weeks, are designed to introduce students to "university-level research and project work." Each is team-taught by one engineering or science faculty member with one nontechnical (humanities or social science or management) faculty member. A limited number of options are offered each year, and all focus on "themes of current global importance." A recent sampling consists of

- Feed the World ... All About Food
- Power the World ... All About Energy
- Grand Challenges ... All About Engineering for Sustainable Development
- Heal the World ... All About Epidemics

Humanities and Arts Requirement. This requires both a "breadth" and a "depth" feature. In the breadth courses, students must take at least one course from two of three "intellectual clusters": one in the fine arts, one more or less in languages and literature, and the other including history, philosophy, and religion. In the depth courses, students must also complete one area of focus, taking at least four courses within one of the three breadth areas. At least one of these courses should be at an advanced level.

The depth component concludes with an inquiry seminar, or practicum, usually during the sophomore year. The purpose of both options is to provide students with a complex exploration of a topic that encourages both independent thought and cooperative learning. Students who choose the practicum option will also be involved in a production and performance component that requires hands-on application of skills and ideas.

Projects. WPI students are required to participate in two significant projects. Students generally plan their interactive qualifying project during the sophomore year and execute it during one or more terms of the junior year. They carry out this project in teams of two to four students who work with one or more faculty advisors to "address a problem that lies at the intersection of science and technology with social issues and human needs." The ideas for these projects often come from external sponsors—for example, a current project cosponsored by the U.S. Department of Agriculture and the Massachusetts Department of Conservation and Recreation to assess the long-term implications of the Asian long-horned beetle infestation—but may also arise from faculty or students. These projects are generally interdisciplinary in nature and consist of at least one unit of academic work—the equivalent of nine credits, or three courses.

The particular terms of major qualifying projects vary from field to field, but generally teams of students work within their majors to define and solve a problem. Once again, this requires at least one unit of work and is the equivalent of three courses. The ability to effectively communicate the results of their work is emphasized.

Global Perspective Program. This program is not necessarily required; nevertheless, about 50 percent of the interactive qualifying projects take place as part of the global perspective program. These occur in project centers specifically designed to prepare students for participation in a globalized world in more than twenty locations worldwide, including Bangkok, Budapest, Hong Kong, Morocco, Japan, France, Panama, Costa Rica, Venice, Namibia, and Silicon Valley. Several components of this program are noteworthy:

- It consists of professional-level projects such as bringing solar power to remote villages in Thailand or assessing the damage to canal walls in Venice.

- In the thirty years since the program's conception, WPI has sent more undergraduate engineering and science students abroad than any other U.S. university.
- The goal of this program is not to provide a traditional study-abroad experience but a deeper level of immersion in local culture.

For more information, go to www.wpi.edu/academics/projects.html.

Green Mountain College, Poultney, Vermont

Green Mountain College's general education model is interesting because of the institution's decision to adopt a campuswide theme, the environment, as an essential component of its identity. Green Mountain is one of the first colleges in the United States to model productive citizenship by achieving climate neutrality. Besides critical thinking, communications, and self-awareness and responsibility, it lists environmental awareness as one of the key components of its general education program. Indeed, the curriculum itself is entitled "The Environmental Liberal Arts." It consists of a combination of core and distribution requirements, although the latter is loosely structured.

The Core. The Environmental Liberal Arts (ELA) core program consists of four courses required of all students:

- Images of Nature. This introductory-level class "explores some of the ways in which human societies make sense of the natural world." It involves
  - A wide range of reading in the natural sciences, literature, and philosophy
  - A focus on writing, including essays and journaling
  - Field trips that both familiarize students with their new home and allow them to explore the application of classroom theories in a real-world setting
  - The start of an ELA portfolio that all students will continue to develop throughout their academic career
- Voices of Community. This first-year writing seminar emphasizes revision and standard writing practices while exploring "how the environment encompasses human relationships and communities."
- Dimensions of Nature. This class focuses on "the development of scientific thought" as humans have come to understand the world around them. At the end of the course, students present carefully researched written and oral projects discussing current scientific work. The research and reading for this course involve a great deal of original scientific

scholarship; consequently, careful analysis of difficult texts is taught in a deliberate manner.

- A Delicate Balance. This capstone course requires that students complete a project relating the course focus to "career projections and goals for civic engagement." The offerings for this course change semester to semester.

Distribution Requirements. In addition to the core courses, students must take seven courses from what Green Mountain College refers to as "distributional categories." Noteworthy here is that there are no particular distributive regulations — that, for instance, a student take X number of math and Y number of humanities courses. Rather, students are "encouraged to find their passion by exploring a diverse range of academic disciplines," which they do by taking one course from each category. The categories provided are

- Quantitative Analysis
- Natural Systems
- Human Systems
- Aesthetic Appreciation
- Moral Reasoning
- Historical Context
- The Examined Life

For more information, go to www.greenmtn.edu/academics/ela.aspx.

PART TWO

GENERAL EDUCATION AT THE COURSE LEVEL

CHAPTER THREE

Designing Effective General Education Courses

General education courses typically have a very different purpose from major courses. Whatever else they may do, major courses are usually intended to prepare students for other courses within their chosen field and for a career involving that field. For that reason, major courses generally seek to teach the knowledge and skills particular to an area so that students can do work within that field.

In contrast, depending on the sort of program an institution might adopt, general education courses can have a wide variety of purposes, ranging from exposing students to different fields, methodologies, or ways of understanding the world to creating opportunities for students to explore the connections and disconnections between different ways of understanding the world.

Two points are crucial here. The first has already been mentioned but bears repeating: the purposes of major courses and the purposes of general education courses are often not the same. That said, a caveat: the purpose *can* be the same if an institution or department chooses to create them that way. But such an approach is likely to create more work for instructors and lead to more frustration—and less productive learning—for students.

The second point is equally important and perhaps just as obvious. The design of every general education course must begin with an understanding of the purpose of the course. How does it fit into the overall goals of the general education curriculum? Related to this, to what extent is that course structure defined at an institutional level? A disciplinary level? A departmental level?

A course level? Answering these questions is key. It's impossible to design a general education course—or any other course for that matter—without knowing how it fits into the bigger picture. Another way of stating this is that planning a course without this information is possible, but it likely won't achieve its stated aims.

THE COURSE CONTINUUM

Once an institution has decided how it would like to design its curriculum, the courses that come out of that structure will fall along a continuum not unlike the distributional-integrative paradigm. On the far left-hand side are standard "101" courses (Figure 3.1). Classes like this require very little explanation: the purpose of Biology 101 (or Sociology 101 or English 101) is to introduce students to the basic concepts and methodologies of the field. The course generally has a standard textbook, with each chapter covering a broad concept or field within the larger topic: cell biology, genetics, marine biology, ecosystems, and so on. For a course of this kind, there will likely be minimal variation from section to section or even institution to institution.

Somewhere in the middle of the continuum are courses that have a distributional philosophy: they're concerned with exposing students to the thinking of the field but with more deliberate attention to matters of integration. Figure 3.2 shows an example of a course from a university in Hong Kong. This course differs from a standard Biology 101 in that it takes a more thematic approach to the field's content. There are several consequences to such a tactic:

- The course will have less breadth. This is not a class that tries to cover every topic related to the field of biology, broadly defined. Nevertheless, it will give students a solid grounding in the methodologies and terminologies of the field.

- The course will allow more depth than a typical Biology 101, going beyond surface-level concepts and exploring in greater detail and more intense application material related to marine biology. Less time spent covering a broad range of topics means more time spent going into depth on the material, providing a higher level of complex thinking and intellectual challenge to students and consequently engaging them more deeply in the course.

- Because this course is not coverage driven, there is greater opportunity to include integrative readings, lectures, discussions, and assignments. Victoria Harbor in Hong Kong is an example of an ecosystem and therefore valuable for teaching the discourse of biology. But like all other ecosystems, it is shaped by public policy (sewage in Hong Kong is only

Figure 3.1. Standard 101 General Education Course

Figure 3.2. Partially Integrated General Education Course

partially treated), business practices (40 percent of the harbor has been reclaimed since the start of the twentieth century), societal assumptions, architectural planning, and so on. Deliberately bringing these factors into the mix or creating assignments that get students to do so provides course participants an excellent opportunity to see the how boundaries among the disciplines are often very fluid.

- This course will foreground the applications of biology and the other areas that students will study, emphasizing the role these fields play in preparing students to meet the challenges of the modern world.

It's worth noting that rather than having a "BIO" or "BIOL" prefix, this course is designated as "GE." Many institutions make the deliberate choice to distinguish courses that are in the general education program from those in the major. The reasons for this are many and relatively obvious, but one unusual consequence in this case is that the designation itself blurs some boundaries. One could assume, to put it another way, that GE 261 is a general course numbering that applies not just to biology but to the other sciences as well and that it might include offerings such as Nutrition in Developing Nations (chemistry) and The Physics of Plant Life. Indeed, a scientist might design a course that blurs multiple areas of science, something that's more difficult when an institution employs traditional "PHYS," "CHEM," and "BIOL" distinctions.

In addition, an approach of this sort may cause students to pay less attention to the designator and more attention to the course topic, possibly

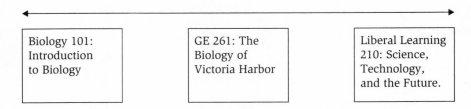

Figure 3.3. A Fully Integrated General Education Course

even circumventing the institutional folklore passed down from year to year (for example, "Biology is harder than chemistry," or "Take physics: it's easy!") and choosing courses based on their personal interests—or even their professional goals.

In Figure 3.3, on the far right-hand side of the continuum, is a course along these lines: Science, Technology, and the Future. At first glance, this may appear to be just another theme-based approach to the sciences. The difference, though, is that a course on this side of the distributive-integrative continuum could be taught by a professor from any field—or, at the very least, a number of different fields. Thus, a professor from physics might teach a course on space programs, a professor from English might teach a course looking at Stephen Hawking and constructions of the future as demonstrated in science-fiction literature, and a professor in sociology might look at industrialism and the poor. Alternatively, a school might choose a lecture-discussion group format (not unlike that used at St. Joseph's; see Chapter Two), wherein students alternate between large lectures by scholars from a variety of fields and meetings with smaller discussion-oriented groups. In each case, the various offerings of Liberal Learning 210 would meet a shared set of standards and expectations and perhaps even practices and assignments. How these expectations were met, however, would vary from field to field.

Implicit within a course of this sort is the necessity of interdisciplinary and interdivisional conversations among faculty. In other words, a class like this could not be effective if the physics professor, the English professor, and the sociology professor didn't each have a sense of what the others were doing and of the degree to which continuity from section to section did or didn't exist. Indeed, in an ideal world, students would be required to take multiple sections of a course of this nature, thereby providing them firsthand experience not just of instructor methods but of the ways in which the various fields tackle topics very differently. Such a requirement would enable some high-end assignments that challenge students to explore how the methodologies of different disciplines vary from one another and the degree to which problem-solving skills from one area can be adapted to another.

Here again, it's important to foreground the fact that as in curricular design, where an institution places general education courses along this continuum will have an impact on both the level and quality of interdisciplinary conversations among the faculty and the degree to which students will have to pursue integration on their own. On the far right-hand side of the continuum, faculty by necessity would be involved in regular conversations with one another to ensure the continuity of course purpose and design. Consequently the courses themselves would probably be more integrative, providing more and better support for students and perhaps allowing them to achieve a more complex and thoughtful degree of synthesis.

In contrast, the middle course concerning Victoria Harbor would likely engender less—and less formal—cross-divisional dialogue. Certainly there may be times when a biology professor approaches a colleague in political science for some ideas on legislative process relative to environmental policy. But by design, a course of this sort is intended to allow an instructor to work within her own field, not so much crossing disciplinary boundaries as unraveling the interdisciplinary strands that already exist within all of our fields.

That said, GE 261 as it is formatted here would certainly necessitate intradivisional conversations. In order to ensure that students across different sections from biology, chemistry, and physics are achieving the same learning goals and being assessed and graded in similar ways, scientists from these different fields would need to have regular formal conversations with one another.

This kind of centrist course design does not necessarily mean students are on their own when it comes to integration. A class like this can be highly integrative in terms of its readings, the lectures and discussions it includes, and the assignments and tests it requires. We'll discuss this more in later chapters, but a single example may suffice. I first encountered the Victoria Harbor course in a workshop at the Hong Kong Institute of Education, the region's premier teacher-training university. Given that all of her students are moving into the field of education on some level (from pre-K to secondary education to administration to government policy), the instructor for a course like this could require her students to design a public education project involving the harbor that does all of the following:

- Incorporates the hard science of the harbor, demonstrating a familiarity with the methodologies of the scientific discipline
- Engages a particular nonscientific audience that is either affected by the harbor or whose actions have consequences for the harbor, or both—for instance, developers who wish to "reclaim" more of the harbor in order to build apartment buildings; government officials who determine sewage treatment regulations; advocates for the tourist industry whose work will be influenced by the level of pollution in the harbor

- Points to a particular problem in the harbor, proposes a solution to this problem, or does both

Key here is the first point: whatever else students do with the content they've learned in the course, they must be able to demonstrate a familiarity with appropriate scientific knowledge and methodologies. Thus, although the evaluation standards for such an assignment would need to be pitched at a level appropriate for introductory-level nonmajors, they should be no lower than in a standard distributional course.

The advantage of courses that lead to an assignment like this is that they make explicit the connections between this course and other courses students will be taking—and indeed, between this course and life. Science, in other words, is no longer something students must learn because breadth is good for them, someday this stuff might be useful to them, or some administrator somewhere decided they should learn this.

The final course design, on the far left of the continuum, Biology 101 (or Sociology 101, or Political Science 101), requires very little conversation among faculty other than possibly department colleagues. It would make sense for an institution taking this approach to have some mechanism—an interdisciplinary committee, perhaps—to ensure a degree of continuity of expectation for all 101 or introductory or distributional courses across the disciplines.

Depending on the design, it's unlikely that there's room within a course of this sort to provide students much support as they consider how one field varies from another. For one thing, a class of this kind is often intent on introducing students to the breadth of a field. For that reason, coverage of content will drive the course, possibly nudging aside integrative assignments like the one described above.

Second, it's not uncommon for a course of this sort to serve simultaneously as a general education requirement and an introduction to the major. When this is the case, including assignments or lectures that are geared to integrative thinking often runs counter to the goal of preparing students to advance in a particular major—or more accurately, faculty teaching these courses often feel the weight of obligation to deliver content to their rising majors, so that students not be found short in upper-division courses.

In situations like this, there are some integrative features that may be augmented in a curriculum in order to aid greater student synthesis of disparate courses. For instance, an institution might require its students to maintain an e-portfolio, including in it not just artifacts from all of their courses, but a series of integrative essays where they explore the ways in which what they've learned in their classes may connect to seemingly unrelated courses.

Similarly, many institutions require projects or senior theses that ask students to pull together their learning from various classes. This is the case at Wagner College in New York, where capstone seminars are designed to "sum up the Wagner student's undergraduate education" (www.wagener.edu/wagner_plan/). It's also the case at Portland State, where capstone courses ask students to "bring together the knowledge, skills, and interests developed to this point through all aspects of their education" (www.pdx.edu/unst/unst-introduction). Similarly, one could argue that both the interactive qualifying projects and the major qualifying projects at Worcester Polytechnic are designed especially to create opportunities for students to draw together the methodologies and content areas they've encountered during their college education.

MAJOR COURSES AS GENERAL EDUCATION COURSES: A CAUTIONARY TALE

Some challenges can arise when introductory major courses double as introductory general education courses. Consider a mildly clumsy metaphor. Say that you're an orchestra conductor, trying to lead your musicians through the intricacies of Mahler's Ninth Symphony, arguably one of the most difficult pieces ever composed. Half of your violinists, cellists, percussionists, and bassists have been trained at Eastman, the Berklee School of Music, and conservatories in Europe. The other half have been playing for only a year. Faced with a mixed orchestra of this sort, be it master musicians and amateurs or major students and nonmajors, an instructor has two choices: teach high to the most knowledgeable students or teach low to the less-knowledgeable students.

Most of us would choose the former. And why not? We know from experience that it's better to set the bar high and demand more from students than to stoop to a lowest common denominator that may help those most lacking but does nothing for the rest. When we have high standards, after all, both the most informed and the least informed are pushed to perform at their highest levels—and therein lies the potential for intellectual growth.

But such an approach can frustrate students who are unfamiliar with the field being discussed and not motivated to become a professional in the field in question. And although it's tempting to say to these students, "Too bad. Life is full of frustrations. Get used to it," the fact of the matter is that a bevy of frustrated students can lead to several unsavory consequences:

- A poisoned classroom in which the learning of all is undermined by the attitudes of a few
- High failure rates
- A lack of actual learning on the part of a large portion of the students enrolled in the class

All of us want to avoid the first of these: our lives are challenging enough without feeling as if we have to strap on armor before marching into our classrooms. And the second of these may seem inconsequential for faculty: it's not our job to ensure that students pass our classes. Indeed, that's their responsibility. But massive numbers of failing students mean wasted resources. When students fail, they have to take the course again. And when lots of students have to take lots of courses over again (and again), that means the institution has to offer a greater and greater number of introductory-level courses, which in today's resource-neutral budgetary environment often means fewer opportunities to offer upper-level major courses.

The third of these consequences — minimal or no learning for a large portion of the students enrolled in our courses — is perhaps a bit more complicated. Again, we may be tempted to say, "Too bad! It's their job to learn! I just provide the material and the opportunities!" And indeed this is actually the case: we can't do our students' learning for them. In order for students to turn our course material into deep learning that will stick with them for years to come, they have to accept responsibility for the material.

But this attitude on our part also begs the question: If we're not that worried about whether our students learn the material, why even require the class? If, in other words, we're willing to live with above-average failure rates and lots of Cs and Ds, aren't we undermining our own rationale for expecting students to take, say, English, biology, or political science as part of their general education distribution requirements? Don't we insist that our courses be made part of our institution's core because we believe that this is material that our students can't — sometimes very literally — live without?

In the end, perhaps it's best to admit that there's something to be said for meeting students where they're at and recognizing that nonmajor and major students need to be approached in different ways. We've long recognized that intrinsic motivation aids learning, and our goal is to teach students and have them learn the material regardless of whether they major in our field. We believe that our fields matter — that knowing something about history or economics or art or mathematics (really knowing, as in being able to recall not just during the test at the end of term, but years from now, when it really matters) makes someone a better citizen, a better employer, a happier person, a more able participant in life.

If this is the case — and I suspect it is for most of us — then a lack of motivation on the part of students can defeat our purposes. And if that's the case, then requiring nonmajor students to take a course designed for more (and differently) motivated major students might be counterproductive. Such a course sends all sorts of messages about the field — about the uses of the field, careers in the field — that don't speak to nonmajors. Perhaps it is better to design separate courses: those that address the needs of students within the major and those that address the needs of students taking the course for general education purposes.

At this point in the conversation, it's not unusual for someone to raise the question, "But doesn't all of this catering to students, trying to appeal to their interests, lead to watered-down, cutesy courses that teach little and waste the time of both faculty and students?"

There's absolutely no reason that this should be the case. The fact that a course is designated as part of an institution's general education curriculum should have no bearing whatsoever on the intellectual and academic demands of the course or the standards by which students are evaluated. This is important enough that it bears repeating: general education should contain intellectually demanding material and push students toward high standards. To expect anything less is an insult to ourselves and our students. Moreover, it defeats the purpose of liberal learning, sending students out into the world without the knowledge and skills they need to survive.

CHAPTER FOUR

How the Purposes of General Education Can Reshape a Course

Case Studies

T he difference between a general education course and a major course covering the same topic is less about what information is provided to students than what students are asked to do with that information.

On one level, this clearly leads to matters of assignment design, a topic discussed in more detail in the next chapter. Suffice it to say for the moment that the kinds of assignments we want to give majors and those we want to give general education students are often very different, particularly if an institution's general education program is more integrative in nature. Although the skills we wish students to demonstrate may be similar in both types of courses, what we're after in an integrative GE course is for students to be able to transfer the course content to other courses and other settings in an effective manner. Certainly students need content, and it must be challenging content, and we do want them to learn the skills and methodologies of our fields. But in the end, the purpose of an integrative course is to make sure that students can take the information they have examined back to their major, back to their home lives, back to their community lives, all in a meaningful way. How might the ability to construct multiple meanings of, say, Christina Rossetti's "Goblin Market," influence their response to Supreme Court rulings

Many thanks to Barbara Tewksbury, whose course design workshop, The Cutting Edge, has shaped much of my thinking here and throughout subsequent chapters.

in a political science course? How can learning the precepts of string theory shape their work in their philosophy major? What can sociology teach an art historian, a poet, or a student studying environmental science?

This goal of transferability influences nearly everything in general education classes. What follows are four and a half case studies that address several of the challenges that arise when designing general education syllabi. All of the courses here are from my home institution because I wanted to be sure I presented these syllabi in a manner that accurately represents the designer's intentions and goals, and working with scholars with whom I had a prior relationship makes this easier. In addition, this approach allows greater continuity, avoiding the need to provide institutional context over and over again. All of the course descriptions are single-instructor, single-field courses, and all of them take a thematic approach to making course content more integrative.

The syllabi in the case studies present effective solutions to the challenges of designing general education courses, but they are not perfect. (Certainly nobody—not me, not their designers—would argue that they are.) The reason is that there is no such thing as a perfect syllabus in the absolute sense. Every syllabus reflects the biases of its creator, the realities—good and bad—of the particular student population to which it is taught, the logistical realities of a ten-week, thirteen-week, or sixteen-week semester, and so on.

The courses described here are less prescriptions than catalysts, included not to end a conversation but to offer the chance to analyze the challenges and opportunities presented by general education—and to get faculty thinking about the variety of solutions that may be available to them as they move forward with their own designs.

CASE STUDY #1: A MAJOR COURSE REVISED INTO AN INTEGRATIVE GENERAL EDUCATION COURSE (BRITISH LITERATURE)

Having a clear sense of purpose can shape the content of a course. This example is from my own field: literature studies. Were I to teach a major course examining British literature from 1800 to the present (a not uncommon offering in universities), I would focus largely on ensuring that students were exposed to the significant writers of this period. I would feel obliged to include at least the following authors:

William Blake   Robert Burns
William Wordsworth   Samuel Taylor Coleridge

John Keats	Percy Shelley
Mary Wollstonecraft	Mary Shelley
At least one of the Brontës	Elizabeth Gaskell
Charles Dickens	George Eliot
Thomas Hardy	Robert Browning
Elizabeth Barrett Browning	Dante Rossetti and the pre-Raphaelites
Christina Rossetti	Oscar Wilde
Virginia Woolf	William Butler Yeats
T. S. Eliot	D. H. Lawrence
Graham Greene	Tom Stoppard

This list, by no means exhaustive, is more or less standard for a survey course for this period. When choosing particular works for each author, I select what I feel best represents them—for example, "Tintern Abby" for Wordsworth and "The Importance of Being Earnest" for Wilde. Or, to be frank, sometimes I make a decision based on what's available in the anthology assigned for the course. I may prefer Barrett Browning's "The Cry of the Children," for instance, but if my textbook doesn't have it, I'll go with (the inevitable) "Sonnets from the Portuguese," figuring that some Elizabeth Barrett Browning is better than none.

And, I'll admit, sometimes I choose a work simply because I can get it to fit. I consider Dickens to be essential reading for this period, but almost all of his novels are incredibly long; *David Copperfield,* for instance, logs in at around nine hundred pages. The exception is *Hard Times,* which is slightly over three hundred pages. The problem is that *Hard Times,* in my opinion, isn't Dickens's best work; it's too didactic and boring on the plot level. But it's short, and I can fit it in, so it will have to do. Similarly, I might go with "The Love Song of J. Alfred Prufrock" as a representative work of Eliot, because it's shorter than *The Waste Land.* Indeed, I would love to include Kate Atkinson's *Behind the Scenes at the Museum,* but I can't find the time. Fourteen (or sixteen, or twelve) weeks isn't enough to cover more than two hundred years of literary evolution.

When I teach a general education course, however, I'm less concerned about the obligation of coverage; there's no intrinsic value in making sure that nonmajor students have read the authors I've listed. Because they're not going on in the major, there is no later course where their lack of familiarity with all of these authors and texts might put them at a disadvantage. Rather, in a general education course, particularly one that's integrative in nature, I'm concerned more about choosing works that might be relevant to my students' lives. So when my institution switched to a theme-based approach to distributional courses, I designed a syllabus that examined the interplay between literature and science and technology (see the syllabus in Appendix A). I've long been fascinated by the perceived split between science and the arts, and I believe that literature students have much to learn from the sciences, and that science students might find much that intrigues them in the arts. My sense was that designing a course on this topic would create a more explicit connection between the supposedly aesthete world of literature and the "real" world. In other words, my hope was that the course would cease to be about art for art's sake (to borrow a pre-Raphaelite phrase) and become a class about how human beings struggle to respond to a rapidly changing world.

The syllabus for this new course came to contain this material:

- William Wordsworth, selected poems, including "The World Is Too Much with Us"
- Samuel Coleridge, selected poems including "Frost at Midnight" and "Kubla Khan"
- Percy Shelley, selected poems, including "Ozymandias"
- Mary Shelley, *Frankenstein*
- Dickens, *Hard Times*
- Elizabeth Barrett Browning, "The Cry of the Children"
- Matthew Arnold, "Dover Beach," "The Buried Life"
- Edgar Allen Poe, "Ode to Science"
- Christina Rossetti, *Goblin Market*
- T. S. Eliot, *The Waste Land*
- Ernest Hemingway, *The Sun Also Rises*
- Martin Heidegger, "The Question Concerning Technology" and "Modern Science, Metaphysics, and Mathematics"
- Selected World War I poets
- Art works by J.M.W. Turner, John Constable, the impressionists, abstract expressionists including Jackson Pollock, and contemporary conceptual artists such as Antony Gormley and Rachel Whiteread
- Hubert Dreyfus, *What Computers Can't Do*
- Philip K. Dick, *Do Androids Dream of Electric Sheep?*

Because I'm not teaching for English majors, I've crossed over into American literature, figuring there was no reason to limit myself arbitrarily. Because I've long been interested in the visual arts and find that visual learning provides a much appreciated respite for word-weary non-English majors, I've included a number of artists whose work demonstrates a deliberate response to the changing world. Similarly, I've included two philosophers whose thinking on modernity and technology strengthens class discussions. The result is a course that is both integrative, making deliberate connections between the arts and sciences, and interdisciplinary, bringing more than one field into the classroom. That the class never requires me to go beyond my own comfort zone is essential, given my busy personal life and the increasing professional demands placed on today's academics.

Beyond that, several points regarding my redesigned course bear mention. First and perhaps most obvious, my selection process when choosing particular works became both simpler and more complicated. It's simpler because I now have a clear set of guidelines when deciding what works to include: whatever I choose must have some connection to matters of science and technological advances. Sometimes this connection is very clear—in *Frankenstein*, for instance, and "Ode to Science." In other works, say, *Goblin Market*, it's more obscure, requiring some carefully worded lectures or questions on my part to wind out the relevant concepts.

At the same time, the selection process becomes more complicated because it requires me to move beyond the massive anthologies that are so prevalent for introductory courses in my field. Thus, instead of simply assigning *The Norton Anthology of British Literature*, Volume II, Sixth Edition, I need to assign seven smaller texts in order to maintain my focus. Although this takes a bit more work in the early stages of creating a course, I at least have the pleasure of knowing that my work in a classroom isn't being determined by the mass-marketing aspirations of a major publisher that knows nothing about my institution, my interests, my students, or the goals of our curriculum.

A second important point about this revised syllabus also relates to matters of text selection: because coverage is less of an issue for nonmajor, general education students, the number of texts I've included is shorter—sixteen, more or less, as opposed to twenty-four in the old syllabus. Consequently, the works are generally longer and more complex. Heidegger challenges almost any undergraduate student, for instance, and *The Waste Land* demands a much higher degree of intellectual engagement than does "Prufrock." What I've done in essence, then, is replace a coverage-style syllabus that forces a fairly superficial approach to the material with a focused address that allows greater depth and more time for reflection and analysis.

This last idea is key: because I'm working with nonmajors, I can't assume a shared discourse relevant to my field on the part of my students. Very likely, I'll need to spend more time in this class (in contrast to a major course) clarifying both terminology and expectations. What exactly do we mean when we talk about "evidence" in a literary discussion? What's the difference between denotation and connotation, and why does it matter? How does one write a thesis when performing literary exegesis? How much liberty is a reader allowed when analyzing a text and the writer's intentions?

Finally, as you may have noticed, this second list still includes *Hard Times,* a novel I've just dismissed as boring and didactic. Given my new focus, though, I included it not because it's conveniently short, but because it says a great deal about how Dickens and Victorian culture struggled with their simultaneous desire to advance the world in a rational way, and their sense, as Mrs. Grandgrind puts it so eloquently, that there must be something more to life than all these "-isms." Indeed, because the course as a whole is focusing on technology, by the time we reach this novel, the class has developed a shared vocabulary that allows a wonderfully complex reading of the work, taking us well beyond Dickens's obvious points into more subtle tensions that we might have otherwise missed.

In short, making the shift from a course designed for majors to a course designed for nonmajors changes everything—even when it doesn't. In the end, thinking about purpose, the audience, and distributional versus integrative approaches makes us more deliberate teachers. Whereas previously I made decisions based on habit, what I experienced in graduate school, or some table of contents designed by a publisher, recognizing the ways in which general education and major courses may differ allows—or causes—me to think more carefully about *my* goals, about *my* students, and about *their* needs.

CASE STUDY #1.5: GENERAL EDUCATION AND COURSE STRUCTURE (BRITISH LITERATURE—AGAIN)

In the same way that general education can liberate us in terms of course content, asking us to be more deliberate when choosing the texts, experiments, and lectures, it can also cause us to rethink the order in which these materials are presented.

For instance, faced with teaching a general education course covering romantic to contemporary literature, I was inclined to design the class following the chronology laid out in my old textbook: romanticism first, then the Industrial Revolution, then modernism, and so on. On occasion I'd cluster materials according to topic, breaking chronology to do several readings on gender roles, for instance. But for the most part, the reading and discussion schedule for my course was determined by some random editor somewhere in New York or London.

And perhaps there's nothing wrong with that. What I realized over time, though, was that this approach put non-English majors at a disadvantage. All of these scientists, mathematicians, economists, and prelaw students walked into my classroom the first session and were told to show up the next day having read a half-dozen poems in antiquated English that described a world and ideas seemingly unfamiliar to the contemporary mind. This is not a bad thing, of course: I enjoy pushing students, forcing them to deal with material that challenges their sensibilities, aesthetic and otherwise. But I found myself spending an inordinate amount of time in the early stages of the course having to teach to multiple purposes on a daily basis. And at the same time that I was providing students with the basic concepts of the field—literary analysis, metaphor, persona, and so on—I was also required to provide historical context and lead complicated discussions about language and meaning. As a result, the literature itself—its themes, meanings, and implications—was almost lost among all the other stuff.

In the end, encouraged by Barbara Tewksbury, a geoscientist whose course design tutorial was originally funded by the National Science Foundation, I made what I then considered an extreme choice: I taught the class backward.

The impact was tremendous. Beginning with the science-fiction classic *Do Androids Dream of Electric Sheep?* (the basis for *Blade Runner*) by Philip K. Dick, I had students who

- Were immediately engaged with the course material
- Didn't have to struggle with sentence-level reading
- Had the energy and time to engage the analytical concepts I was introducing
- Came to class with examples from movies, books, and their lives that related to our reading
- Felt like old hands with literary analysis by the time they got to the end of the course and were thus less intimidated by the older texts that are more difficult to read

One unanticipated consequence was the way that Dick's novel ended up providing a metaphor—what it means to be human versus what it means to be an android—that we carried with us throughout the course, applying similar questions to Hemingway, Dickens, and Mary Shelley. In all my years of teaching literature, I don't remember an operative metaphor of this sort being brought forward from the older works to the contemporary reading.

Lost, of course, was the way in which an earlier period can influence a later one, either negatively or positively. Here again, though, this is less of a concern—if it's a concern at all—with this particular population. In contrast to the major, this isn't the purpose of the course. And to the extent that this knowledge might be useful, a mini-lecture about an earlier period generally sufficed. Indeed, mention of an era prior to covering that period can prime students for more effective learning later because the relevant topics of a course are covered more than once, reinforcing the neural networks coding the knowledge.

My point here is not to teach every course backward; rather, it's that thinking about purpose can often free us up in terms of structure, causing us to be more deliberative, creative, and ultimately successful in our teaching. For instance, a course might also be taught in terms of a number of clusters, with three primary texts—say, *Do Androids Dream of Electric Sheep? Hard Times,* and *Frankenstein*—at the center of the course, and all of the other works read on a secondary level, mainly to inform the class's understanding of these major pieces. Rather than appearing as a list, then, the course can be visualized as a series of three clusters, with the key works at the center and all of the others orbiting around them. Figure 4.1 is an example of this, drawn from the first cluster of the course, with Dick's novel at the center.

An approach like this highlights the connections between the works rather than the chronological order in which the works appeared or the order in which a textbook places them. In practical terms, it also changes the rhythm of a class: rather than reading a central text in a concentrated period of time (say, two class sessions for Dick's work), this approach allows a text to be read in sections spread out over a few weeks and intermingled with some of the other pieces that help in understanding it. Not only can this lead to more effective learning, contextualizing smaller ideas alongside larger works, it helps students unused to lots of reading learn to pace themselves.

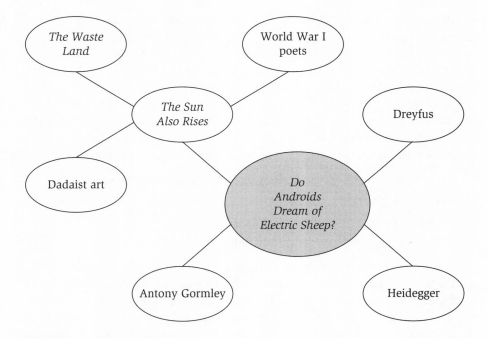

Figure 4.1. Clustering Texts

Alternatively, an instructor might structure a course around a series of case studies, providing students with the information to solve a particular scholarly problem on a need-to-know basis. This method, sometimes referred to as "just-in-time" pedagogy, is built around the theory that deep learning is more likely to occur with immediate application of course content. Certainly this makes more sense than a course in which students are asked to be passive all term and then, during the last two weeks of the semester, are suddenly required to be active thinkers.

Here again, though, the point is not that there are two or three ways to construct a syllabus that are better than all other approaches. Rather, my argument is that when we pay close attention to the purposes of general education courses, we often begin to see alternative structures that may allow for more effective learning.

CASE STUDY #2: GENERAL EDUCATION AND COURSE STRUCTURE, CONTINUED (PHYSICS)

But enough about literature. "Maybe," I've heard many scientists say, "you can get away with that kind of stuff in the humanities. In my field, though, it's different."

Okay, so what about fields where, say, covering the course content backward might lead to disaster? Is an instructor teaching a general education course to nonmajors then forced to adhere to the textbook's table of contents?

The simple answer is no. Consider, as an example, a general education course redesigned by Rama Balasubramanian and Bonnie Price, two of my colleagues in physics. Given the choice between a basic Physics 101 for nonmajors and rethinking a class in terms of deep-sea and sky diving, they chose the latter. (For a full copy of this syllabus, see Appendix B.)

In its previous configuration, Price's class took a fairly standard approach:

- Unit A: Force, Newton's laws of motion, and scientific theories
- Unit B: Light, sight, and rainbows
- Unit C: Heat, temperatures, and cloud formation
- Unit D: Buoyancy, pressure, and flight

These topics were presented sequentially, following the sequence in the textbook. In a typical term, only two or three of these topics could be covered, and the course as a whole seemed random, at least to the students, with one topic following another with no clear connection. Certainly connections could be made—say, between units A and D—but according to Balasubramanian, the physics faculty "always thought about tying the concepts together through a common theme.'' The topic of sky diving and deep-sea diving was chosen because it allows discussion of a large portion of the topics listed above and it presents these topics in a real-world context that is tangible to students.

For the redesigned course, faculty chose motion as the main theme. The revised course is structured as follows:

Unit 1 — Sky Diving: The Motion of Objects Under the Influence of Forces

- Embedded topics: Concepts of position, velocity, acceleration, force, air resistance, friction, static and kinetic frictional forces.

In this unit, students come to understand the concept of motion by performing a set of experiments that answer questions such as these:

- How do forces affect the motion of an object that is moving in a line?
- What is the difference between uniform motion and nonuniform motion?
- What is a free-fall motion?
- How is the motion of an object affected by gravity and friction?

Unit 2 — Deep Sea Diving: The Motion of Objects Under Water

- Embedded topics: Concepts of force, pressure, buoyancy, density, specific gravity, Archimedes principle, Bernoulli's theory.

Here, students explore questions relating to the factors affecting underwater motion by addressing the following essential questions in a lab setting:

- Why do some objects sink while others float?
- How do gases respond to external forces?
- What is pressure?
- Using pressure and equilibrium, can we build a machine that can lift very heavy objects with very little effort?
- How does pressure differ at various locations in air and water?
- What role does pressure difference play in enabling birds and airplanes to fly?

A quick scan of the topics listed for the original Physics 101 and this course shows that deep-sea and sky diving essentially focus on units A and D from the original syllabus, with bits and pieces of unit C thrown in where they relate to the topic of motion. Given that the old course was never able to cover more than three of the four units in the best-case scenario, the worst-case scenario means there's a net loss here of roughly half of a unit.

What is gained, though, is a sense of unity that allows students to build one idea on another. Whereas in the Physics 101 construction of the syllabus, force, light, and heat were all taught, there was no sense of how they related to one another. This is not a minor detail: cognitive neuroscience tells us that it is always easier to teach a person new information if he or she is able to connect it to prior knowledge (Mantyla, 1986). Established neural networks are stronger than newer networks; therefore, if the new information can be connected to the old, it becomes easier to access.

All of this relates to the concept of integration: if we can integrate course content by connecting it to other classes the students have taken, experiences they've had in their lives outside class, or even just the very concrete image of a body hurtling toward the earth, there's a better chance that this content will become part of a student's deep learning; she will then be able to access that information sometime in the future when she needs it. And that, after all, is why we require these courses: to prepare students for future challenges.

CASE STUDY #3: A DUAL-PURPOSE COURSE REDESIGNED AS A GENERAL EDUCATION COURSE (SOCIOLOGY)

The two examples in this section are from the field of sociology. As is not uncommonly the case at institutions that haven't revised their general education curriculum, this first iteration of Sociology 101 is a dual-purpose course, serving as both a distribution option for nonmajors and the required gateway course for potential majors. In its original form, the purposes of Introduction to Sociology were stated in this way:

Upon successful completion of the course, students will be able to

- Explain the major theories and research methods used in sociology
- Apply some basic sociological concepts
- Begin to use a sociological perspective to examine everyday life
- Apply their sociological imagination to understand social inequality

Topics covered in this course included as extensive an overview of the field as is possible in a thirteen- or fourteen-week semester, including most of the following:

Stratification	Social control
Theoretical perspectives	The history of sociology
Education	Family
Politics/power	Religion
Gender	Race
Social class	Groups
Deviance	Culture
Socialization	Population
Collective behavior	

As with the British literature course, the key driver here is the sense that students need to be exposed to the field as a whole. Majors need this, the logic goes, because it allows them to determine if this is indeed the field they wish to pursue and this initial survey prepares them for more in-depth learning.

I'll leave any discussion of the majors and major courses to professors in each field; they know their students and the demands of their profession. My concern here is with the nonmajors who take a course like this or similar dual-purpose courses in other fields. For these students, the prevailing logic argues that because this is their only exposure to sociology (or whatever other field), they need a course that emphasizes breadth and coverage so that they can learn as much as possible in the short time available.

This logic is reinforced in the language of the course goals I've included here: students will be expected to explain all of the major theories of the field. In addition, there's an implicit recognition within this language that quality and depth of learning are being traded for quantity of content: students will be expected to apply some basic concepts and begin to use sociological perspectives. Notably, the major assessment and evaluation methods for the course are four exams worth 20 percent each. The only project for the course is a review of a sociological text, and it is worth less than any one of the exams. The key here is coverage and content: get it all out, hit all of the chapters in the book, and make sure students have encountered everything—even if they haven't necessarily used it.

What all of this overlooks is that just because students have been taught a subject doesn't mean they've learned it (Gaston, 2010c). Indeed, if we've learned anything in recent years about how the brain takes in information and turns it into deep learning, it's that mere exposure, through lectures or discussion, is not enough. (See Rhodes, 2010; Clark, 2010; and Zull, 2002, particularly the third chapter dealing with brain connections that change "data" into "knowledge.") Thus, a political science major who takes an Introduction to Sociology course like the one outlined above might perform well enough on the exams to receive an A and might leave the course three months later entirely convinced that sociology has nothing to teach him. Information has been delivered, yes, but if no connections are made—if, as Gaff and Ratcliff (1997) put it, knowledge is not acted on—the details will disappear as soon as the final exam is over.

This is a bleak picture, of course, and a bit of an exaggeration. Many nonmajors do find some connection with the course—some component that engages or charms them and that they recognize as relevant to their lives. It's sociology, after all, and as a friend of mine in the field likes to say, "Sociology is everywhere."

But I'm going to assume that what we're after in the classroom is more than just random chance that the occasional student will have an aha! moment. If we believe that our fields matter enough to nonmajors that they be required to take them, then we want to universalize those moments of success as much as possible, creating a deeper and more applied learning that will last and be accessible and useful for years to come, regardless of a student's chosen career path.

That in mind, the two syllabi I present are explicit in their movement away from coverage for coverage's sake, choosing instead thematized approaches to the field that are both more focused and more aggressive in their integration. Both courses are part of a strands model described in Chapter Two: courses from different fields are clustered within a loose category to enable greater integration. The first course, Traveling Without Leaving, fits under a global strand (see Appendix C for a full copy of this syllabus, designed by Meeta Mehrotra of Roanoke College, Salem, Virginia). The goals of the syllabus state that on completion of the course, students will be able to

- Describe some of the global variation in cultural practices and social institutions
- Communicate effectively about global variations in cultural practices and social institutions in an oral format
- Describe the methodologies that sociologists use
- Explain how social forces shape individuals
- Write clearly and effectively about the impact of social forces in their own lives
- Articulate how the course's global perspective is reflected in the course content

A few points here bear mention. First, these goals are much less general than those presented for the Sociology 101 syllabus. Students are expected to know and understand sociological theories, but mainly in the context of globalization and global variation. Second, these new goals more likely match the ideals of the instructor; they express, in other words, her highest hopes for her students in the course, not a lowest-common-denominator approach. And as Robert Diamond (2008) points, out, starting with less than our highest ideals can result in an inferior course. Third, there's an emphasis here on writing and speaking about social theories and social forces. In part, this is a consequence of an institution-specific requirement that all general education courses address two of the following competencies: written communications, oral communications, and quantitative reasoning. Readers at institutions that don't have requirements like these should ignore them. At the same time, though, it may be useful to note that these competencies—I'm avoiding the word *skills*, which seems reductive—add to better learning of course materials. I discuss this topic more in Part Three of this book, but basically, writing about, speaking about, or using quantitative reasoning to address a topic leads to greater processing of that topic and likely stronger neural networks relating to that topic—and hence, greater access to the information should it become necessary to retrieve at a later date.

The topics covered in this course are less general in nature, more particularly defined than in the generic 101 syllabus. They include

- The importance of globalism
- Methods of social research
- The influences of culture on the individual
- The impact of economics
- Social constructions of gender
- A comparative analysis of family

Quite obviously, the number of content items listed here is much shorter than the number listed in the generic 101 syllabus—six as opposed to seventeen. In practical terms, this means that each item receives more attention, more time in the classroom, and more reading outside the classroom. This is a simple matter of math: fewer topics in the same finite time period mean more time per topic. In contrast to the Sociology 101 syllabus, where no single topic receives more than a week of class time, students who take Traveling Without Leaving spend two full weeks examining the influences of culture on the individual and two and a half weeks looking at the impact of economics. More time on a topic, of course, means greater depth; greater depth means more detail; and more detail, I would assert, means greater complexity.

And complexity and detail are important. Research seems to indicate that it leads to better, deeper learning (Roediger and Karpicke, 2006). When we're forced by coverage concerns to provide students with a minimal amount of information on a given topic—say, social constructions of gender—we're limited in what we can ask them to do with that information on a cognitive level. I'm thinking of Bloom's taxonomy here, a not unproblematic paradigm, I know, but one that is nonetheless useful for this discussion. Bloom essentially argues that there are low-end cognitive skills and high-end cognitive skills. At the low end are actions like listing, repeating, describing, and paraphrasing. At the high end are skills like appraising, constructing, defending, and synthesizing. Given a limited understanding of a topic—say, a basic vocabulary and several relevant examples—it might be difficult for a student to synthesize two seemingly disparate concepts or to evaluate the pluses and minuses of competing ideas in a sophisticated way. In *The Art of Changing the Brain*, James Zull discusses the distinction between experts and novices:

> Whether we are an expert or a novice, our brains basically sense the same things. The difference is that the expert knows which part of his sensory data is important

and which part isn't. The brain of the chemist knows that the *prime* (in a chemical formulation) is important, but the size of the delta isn't. The chemistry novice, on the other hand, sees every little thing as being of equal value [p. 141].

While it would be foolish to argue that spending two weeks on a topic instead of one week will necessarily make a student an expert instead of a novice, it's not far-fetched to say that an added week nevertheless allows significant movement away from raw novice, particularly when those two weeks are intrinsically connected to what was learned the two weeks before that, and the two weeks before that, and the two weeks before that. In other words, in a thematically focused course of this sort, the learning of a single content area isn't isolated from everything else that the student learns: the information learned in the third week can help a student better understand the information encountered in the seventh week, which in turn can help the student understand the information presented in the eleventh week. This cumulative effect leads to greater understanding and greater attention to detail, which allows students to present—and us to expect—more complex arguments when synthesizing, evaluating, and so on. This isn't necessarily the case in many coverage-based courses, where the topics presented in the fifth week (say, marine biology) aren't necessarily related to those in the twelfth week (say, the human genome) or where the connections that do exist are so intricate and obscure as to make using one topic to inform another infeasible.

The second redesign of Sociology 101 also takes a focused, thematic approach to the field (see Appendix D for a full copy of this syllabus, designed by Diane V. Brogan of Roanoke College). Entitled "Elite Deviance," it states as its course goals that students who have completed the class should be able to

- Identify the nature of elite deviance as well as its social costs and consequences
- Analyze the role of power, privilege, and wealth in this social problem
- Critically evaluate the conditions and social arrangements that precipitate elite deviance and affect society's response to it
- Predict what social changes would be needed to reduce the incidence of this behavior significantly
- Synthesize, critique, and summarize material effectively in order to communicate more succinctly verbally and in writing

The goals of this course are even more narrowly focused than in the previous example: everything here relates directly to the concept of elite deviance. More explicit here too is the connection between oral and written communications and critical thinking. Writing and speaking in this syllabus is more than just a skill: it's a means of deepening one's understanding of the course material.

Not surprisingly, the topics covered in this syllabus vary from the travel course. Students enrolled in this section work with

- Stratification and inequality
- Social control
- Theoretical perspectives
- Culture
- Politics
- Gender

Many of the same arguments that I made about the Traveling Without Leaving syllabus can be made here as well: there's more focus to the reading, and thus more depth, which arguably allows more complex forms of learning. Furthermore, both syllabi are intensely integrative in nature. Like the original Sociology 101 syllabus, they seek to have students apply the social theories they learn to everyday life. Beyond that, these courses make explicit connections to other fields. With its focus on globalism, the travel course will have clearly visible benefits for students studying literature, art, psychology, business, politics, and international affairs, to name just a few areas. With its focus on class and crime, the elite deviance course has direct application for students studying psychology, criminal justice, business, journalism, and politics. This is not to say that a general sociology course doesn't also carry these integrative features: it does. Sociology—like biology, political science, literature, and nearly every other field we require as part of a distributive model—touches almost every corner of our lives. The point here is that these syllabi are deliberately designed to foreground these connections, to make this integrativeness—and not a broad coverage of the field—the driving purpose of the course.

One real benefit here is that both courses allow professors to teach topics that connect to their own professional and personal lives. This is good, of course, because intrinsic motivation isn't a factor just for students. When we teach a topic that we care about deeply (not to mention one that we've studied extensively), we're more likely to bring a higher level of engagement not just into the classroom but into the time we spend preparing for the course, responding to students' papers, creating tests, and so on. And while pleasure is sometimes frowned on in our field, it should be noted that burned-out, cynical, tired, and disengaged faculty benefit no one—especially not the students.

But this is about more than creating "fun" courses: none of this requires sacrificing the learning of students. There is no absolute law that says that a student who hasn't read X author or Y theory should not be allowed into society. (And even to the extent that we may believe X and Y must be learned, we certainly have the ability to develop an approach that includes them.) Indeed, by creating a course that allows more depth, we've created an environment in which we can demand more complex thinking from students.

CASE STUDY #4: REDESIGNING A GENERAL EDUCATION SERVICE COURSE (STATISTICS)

For a lot of fields, particularly in the natural and social sciences, the study of statistics is a requirement. At some institutions, the department that imposes this requirement might have a statistician on staff who teaches a field-specific course: thus, there are statistics courses specifically for the social sciences or even just for individual fields. At many institutions, though, staffing is such that this solution isn't feasible. At these places, statistics will be taught by the mathematics department, and any given section will be filled with students from a variety of majors, including biology, political science, sociology, and economics. Often this course will also fulfill a general education requirement. Moreover, the successful completion of a course like this will be one of the factors taken into consideration for students who apply for graduate school.

As a result, the content for a course like this is nonnegotiable: these basics of statistical analysis must be covered:

- Qualitative versus quantitative data
- Graphical methods
- Variability
- Standard deviation
- Outliers
- Probability
- Unions, intersections, and complements
- Distributions
- Regression
- Intervals
- Proportions

The key to designing an integrative course that manages to cover all of these topics is to remember that statistics is required by so many majors because it's key to those majors. Put another way, statistics is required because it's everywhere. What an instructor must do, then, is choose a topic narrow enough to allow an effective level of integration but broad enough to allow coverage of all of the necessary topics.

The first course I'm presenting, Does Gun Control Save Lives? designed by Chris Lee of Roanoke College, is a case in point (see Appendix E for the syllabus). As Lee points out, the question that drives the course is broad and ambiguous:

- What is meant by *gun control?*
- Are certain types of guns restricted?
- Is ownership restricted?
- Is gun control a federal, state, or municipal issue?
- What defines a "saved" life? Are we talking just about a home owner or other would-be victim here, or does the life of the criminal count?
- Does the gun have to be actually fired in an incident for a life to be saved, or should the mere presentation of a firearm be considered prevention?
- If a home or car or business is entered and a gun seems to prevent further violence, do we count as "saved" the lives of everyone present in the home or business or car, or just the person holding the gun?

What looks like a simple question really isn't. As a result, there's more room for statistical analysis, more case studies to examine, more ambiguity that students must deal with. And as any mathematician will tell you, dealing with ambiguity and developing interpretation are essential skills when dealing with numbers, not to mention language (Chris Lee, e-mail to the author, June 28, 2011). In this way, the course is broad enough that it allows all of the standard statistical terms and practices to be dealt with in a contextualized manner.

In another course, Statistics and Botany, Adam Childers foregrounds the relationship of plants, plant growing, and mathematics (see Appendix F). Subjects like probability and outliers, unions, intersections, and random variables are dealt with in the context of matters of plant reproduction; distribution, in all its glorious forms, is explored amid the study of farming and food growing.

Everything I've noted about the other syllabi applies here: instructors are offered the opportunity to teach the topics that drive their own work; students are given the chance to see the relevance of what they're studying. Lee puts it this way (e-mail to the author, June 28, 2011):

In a typical intro stat course, the material is plowed through in a linear direction. Each chapter will incorporate examples to illustrate the topic, but there is rarely a common theme to the applications. The content is primary, the application secondary and unorganized.

In [the redesigned course] we tried to reverse this. Each course has a theme or question. The pursuit of an answer to the question motivates the study of the material. From the beginning students see that we need statistics to answer questions and make decisions.

In other words, students experience firsthand the reality that they must learn statistics to understand the world around them. In this way, "Stat" ceases to be a random requirement and becomes a powerful tool for thinking critically about questions that matter. By integrating content with methodology, meaning is made.

The very fact that a course like this cannot narrow its coverage actually works to the benefit of an instructor seeking to redesign, forcing her to examine the real-world applications—the ways in which the course material really matters in other fields—and construct a course that makes these connections clear.

PART THREE

GENERAL EDUCATION AT THE ASSIGNMENT AND ASSESSMENT LEVEL

CHAPTER FIVE

Designing Appropriate Assignments for General Education

In his seminal work, *Engaging Ideas* (2011), John C. Bean discusses what he calls "the traditional way to assign writing," in which students are encouraged to hand in a paper on "any aspect of the course that interests you," pending the approval of the professor. Bean describes what usually happens next:

> About halfway through the term, students submit proposals for topics—usually stated as a topic area rather than as a research question or tentative thesis. The instructor either approves the topic or advises that it be narrowed or otherwise refined.... At the end of the term, the teacher collects and grades the papers. Some teachers mark the papers copiously; others make only cryptic end comments. Much to the teachers' disappointment, many students never pick up their papers from the teacher's office [pp. 89–90].

There is nothing intrinsically wrong with this sort of generic research essay. Indeed, this approach may be exactly what's needed for advanced students in a major course where intrinsic motivation is high and it seems safe to assume that somewhere in the syllabus is a topic that interests every student.

It's worth considering, however, the ways in which this kind of assignment might not be as productive as we'd hope, particularly in the context of general education. Consider:

- *Papers like this don't necessarily fit the goals of our general education courses and programs.* Although assigning a research paper with an extensive literature review makes sense in a major course, particularly at an advanced

75

level, general education courses are often driven by a different sense of purpose. And just as the purpose of a course can change the structure of that course, so too can it—indeed, should it—reshape the kinds of work students do in a general education class. If one purpose of a general education course in, say, sociology, is to get students to explore the connections between economic class, deviance, and their own fields, why have them look into the narrowly focused and often esoteric research and writing of a bunch of sociology professors? If the purpose of the course is to expose students to the language and methodologies of the field of chemistry, is an extensive and very difficult literature review necessarily the best way to do that?

That said, it should be noted that research is a skill that can be invaluable in the workplace and that, like all other complex skills, needs to be taught not just once in a student's academic career, but repeatedly and at increasingly complex levels. Therefore, it's incumbent on every institution going through a curricular revision to think about research methods: where they are being taught, by whom, and how often. And if a particular college or university decides that research methods should be one of the goals of the general education curriculum, then assigning papers that include it is a must—though preferably not in the generic format that Bean decried.

• *Are research methods being taught in the course?* Research methodologies are complex and need to be taught deliberately, and this takes time. If learning research methods is one of the intended outcomes for students of a general education course, then requiring one or more research papers makes perfect sense—assuming the instructor is willing to take the class time to teach these skills, and teach them repeatedly. If this is not the case, however, then, grading students on their ability to do a literature review at the university level is inappropriate unless it has been taught repeatedly in previous courses, and requiring research from students will detract from the actual goals of the course, including the kinds of learning that we're actually after.

• *Papers like this are easy to plagiarize.* Assignments that are broadly defined and provide few guidelines can be downloaded from the Internet in a matter of minutes. Even assigning multiple drafts of a paper cannot deter this practice: all a student need do is rough up the downloaded paper, turning it in as a first draft, then hand in the original version as the ''final'' copy. Beyond the obvious ethical questions this raises, it's also worth pointing out that writing is a means of developing greater familiarity with a topic—and that plagiarism, large or small, inhibits learning.

• *Assignments like this can lead to ''data dumps'' and less effective learning.* This term also comes from John Bean (2011), who describes a relatively new college student, ''not yet at home with academic writing,'' who ''patches together quotes, statistics, and other raw information without a thesis or coherent organizational plan." In short, the student takes all of the information he has "researched" (for example, found on the Internet) and "dumps" it on the reader's desk (pp. 22–23, 75). We've all seen papers like this in which the student strings together a series of block quotations with generic transitions and cobbles it all with a wobbly thesis along the lines of, "There are many ways of looking at the legalization of marijuana," or "Hamlet was a complex guy." Data dumps require very little from students in terms of their thinking: they must simply be able to locate sources (usually, again, using a general search engine), summarize them, and cite them appropriately. Even evaluating these sources is kept to a fairly minimal level. When students resort to this kind of approach for a research paper, instructors see little evidence regarding students' ability to think. A paper that's 90 percent quotations doesn't allow any instructor to evaluate how much the student has learned, how subtle and complex her reasoning is, or the ways in which the instructor might adapt her teaching to attain greater results.

- *Students seldom enjoy writing these papers.* We know that intrinsic motivation counts for a lot when it comes to learning, which is why we encourage students to choose a topic of their liking. An approach like this, though, assumes that students have found the class as a whole engaging and that they've developed a particular interest in a particular topic. Sometimes this is the case, particularly in elective courses or major courses. In a required general education course, however, this assumes a great deal—though this book and others like it certainly seek to address that issue.

- *We seldom enjoy grading these papers.* This can vary, of course, depending on the kind of institution you're at, the types of students your college is able to recruit, and so on. And even in some of the roughest semesters we might have, occasionally there'll be a bright student who really stumbles on something he cares about and consequently creates inspired work or works really hard no matter what class she's in.

I once visited a school where every general education course required a three-thousand-word final paper. In a course with twenty-five students (a fairly low enrollment, it's worth noting), that means seventy-five thousand words, or roughly three hundred pages of undergraduate writing—not a bad length when you're reading the latest best seller, but another story altogether when we're talking about a group of young scholars struggling to find their way from novice to expert in the course of a single semester.

That said, what we need, then, is a way to design assignments that will ensure higher-order thinking, pushing students away from summary and paraphrase toward synthesis, construction, and application, and finally, the kinds of insights that will engage them as writers and us as readers. That sounds like a tall order, but it's not.

In the end, what we're after when we create assignments (and, for that matter, essay exams) for general education courses is student work that

- Provides evidence that students are learning what we want them to — for example, achieving the stated purposes of the general education program
- Engages students in learning that will be long lasting
- Doesn't make us cry when we read it

That last point might sound a bit glib, but it's quite serious. We didn't get into this profession to be babysitters and bean counters; we became scholars and professors because we believe that ideas matter and that the work we do is important in creating a better world. Whatever assignments we design for students should create a genuine dialogue between them and us about things that matter.

CREATING A MORE PRODUCTIVE RHETORICAL AUDIENCE

Paradoxically, one of the ways to get more scholarly thinking and writing from students is to move their work into a less scholarly context. When conceptualizing the act of writing — or of speaking, or even test taking — it helps to consider Figure 5.1, one variation on Aristotle's conceptualization of the rhetorical context. In this construction, changing any one of the three points of the triangle will change everything. Say a student wishes to write an e-mail to her grandmother about a party she went to. In the course of that communication, she will likely construct the writer (herself) as a responsible participant in the event. As she discusses the party (the topic), she will probably leave out some of the more salacious details for fear of offending her nana, deliberately omitting mention of large quantities of alcohol, "hotties," or "hookups." If she instead addressed the e-mail to her best friend from high school — in other words, a different audience — these same bawdy details might dominate the missive. Indeed, wouldn't that be the whole point of writing? Similarly, our student would be less concerned about constructing herself in a positive way; she might indeed go so far as to exaggerate her own role in the bacchanal — perhaps writing, "I was sooooo *wasted!*"

In other words, changing the audience changes everything. In the same way, changing the topic also has an impact on everything else. Consider, for example, how an e-mail from the same student to the same high school friend would be very different if it were about attending the funeral of a mutual acquaintance.

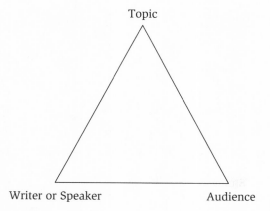

Figure 5.1. The Rhetorical Triangle

It's obvious that as professors, we have the power to manipulate the rhetorical context: we can change the topic, the audience, and even the writerly roles that we ask students to assume. Now look at Aristotle's rhetorical triangle, configured this time along the lines of the traditional generic research paper (Figure 5.2).

Given the imbalance relative to the course content between the writer and the audience in this scenario, I'm tempted to draw the triangle in a different way, attaching a handle to the top of it and turning it into a dagger, making explicit the danger and risk a student perceives as he stares up at his instructor

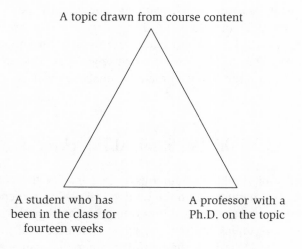

Figure 5.2. The Rhetorical Triangle Configured for a Traditional Research Paper

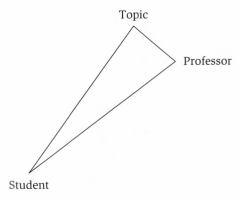

Figure 5.3. The Rhetorical Triangle from the Perspective of a Student

and up at this topic: because the professor, of course, knows the topic very well and is gazing down at the student, grade book in one hand and red pen in the other (Figure 5.3). No wonder students recoil into data dumps—it can't be wrong if it's research!—or even plagiarism. That students are able to write at all in such a rhetorically loaded situation is a miracle. This rhetorical situation, of the "amateur" student writing or speaking to the "professional" scholar, likely accounts for all of those jargon-laden essays we receive. Students, fearing they can't measure up in terms of knowledge, do their best to at least sound as if they're part of the academic discourse community. (See, for instance, Bartholomae, 1985.)

What we're after, then, particularly in a general education context where students are likely encountering relatively new information, is a way of reconfiguring the state of affairs so that we can create not necessarily a more level playing field but a more accurate one, where students aren't so overwhelmed by audience that they find themselves incapable of showing what they do know about a topic, not to mention unable to engage in higher-order thinking.

CONSIDERING SOME ALTERNATIVES

One helpful way of thinking about this is to consider the consequences a particular audience might have on the writing task. What audiences will allow a writer to coast because there's an assumption of shared knowledge and familiarity with the topic? In contrast, what audiences will push a student to explain complex ideas in a thoughtful manner that can lead not just to understanding by the reader but mastery by the writer?

Jane Danielewicz and Jordynn Jack (2009) of the University of North Carolina, Chapel Hill, have constructed three categories that create a useful way of thinking about the relationship between writers and audiences:

1. *Insider-to-insider situations.* The assumption is that both the writer and the audience are very familiar with the topic. As a result, insider-to-insider writing uses more field-related jargon and may often leave foundational ideas unexplained (or briefly explained) because writer and reader have shared knowledge. For example, an advanced art history major writing a proposal to her advisor as part of a senior project will not need to define what she means by the rhythm of a piece. Both reader and writer will understand.

2. *Insider-to-nonspecialist situations.* The audience here is generally knowledgeable in the discipline but not necessarily an expert on the topic at hand. A chemist writing a National Science Foundation grant proposal would want to think about a nonspecialist audience, for example, knowing that her readers might not be fully versed in her particular branch of chemistry—indeed, might even be from the fields of biology or physics. In this case, there is some shared discourse and similar levels of professional engagement, but more than basic information—and likely more explanation of that information—will be necessary for a successful communication experience.

3. *Insider-to-public situations.* When writing to a public audience, students can assume very little foundational knowledge on the part of their readers. As a result, they must carefully explain every term, every concept, and every idea. An example of this kind of rhetorical situation is a letter to the editor of a local paper or even an article in a popular magazine like *Time* or *Newsweek.*

I've included this typology to make the point that as instructors, we have options available when we design assignments and projects for students. Although the insider-to-insider approach might be fine for some students in some situations—say, advanced undergraduates—in a general education context, it often can perform a disservice to both our students and ourselves. Even the best students may struggle to assume the mantle of expertise, filling their essays with off-the-mark jargon and glossing over complex ideas in simplified ways. And we may find ourselves reading a stack of essays that skate along the surface and fail to give us a sense of how much the students have learned.

The situation is exacerbated in general education courses where "insider-to-insider" might more accurately be described as "outsider-to-insider." In this way, assigning traditional research papers where students are asked to locate, read, and add their voices to densely written research of the top scholars in a field is little more than a polite lie between friends: students with other majors pretend that they are scholars on par with professors with Ph.D.s in the field, and the professors pretend not to notice that their "colleagues" are only nineteen years old, carrying skateboards, and studying in another discipline entirely.

In contrast, shifting to an insider-to-nonspecialist or insider-to-public approach creates a situation in which students can stop pretending by, ironically, pretending to write to someone other than the professor—more specifically, to someone whose knowledge level on the topic is more on par with or even below the students' own.

One major consequence of this approach is that it forces students to explain ideas, terminology, and concepts carefully: no longer can they gloss over their logic or assume the audience's familiarity with key ideas from the text or a lecture. Writing to readers who are unfamiliar with the topic requires a kind of "translation" on the part of the student author. On the simplest level, they must take complex terminology that is understood within the field and explain it in a way that the average audience can understand: What exactly is a neural network? What do artists mean when referring to *chiaroscuro*? How does "narrator" differ from "persona"? At a more complex level, this translation involves the explanation of intricate ideas: What exactly is the Hawthorne effect? The Stark law? What does a conceptual artist mean when she says she wants to create a space for silence?

I once heard a psychology professor describe the various levels of memory available to the human mind. The shallowest form, he said, went something like this. You're walking along, reading a newspaper. You recognize that there's a person moving toward you on the pathway and that the two of you might bump into one another. Passing this person, you pay just enough attention to avoid a collision. Two minutes later, when you're asked the gender of this person, you have no idea. Similarly, shallow summary and data dumping require little else of our students than a casual glance as they copy words from one place to another. The information passes into shallow memory and then disappears again almost immediately. Learning, if it exists at all, will be minimal.

In contrast, when a student must explain a concept using his or her own words in a situation where it matters—for example, to an audience who is uninformed rather than to a professor who is an expert—a greater degree of cognitive processing is required and will lead to deeper learning. Cognitive neuroscientist James Zull (2002) asserts that deep learning must involve both the front and back of the brain's cortex, engaging both reflection and action: "Data enters learners through concrete experience where it is organized and rearranged through reflection. But it is still just data until learners begin to work with it. When learners convert this data into ideas, plans, and actions ... things are now under their control. They have created and are free to continually test their own knowledge" (p. 40).

Key here is the distinction between data and knowledge. It's one thing to gather a lot of factoids (Zull goes on to point out that we live in the "information age," not the "understanding age"). It's another thing to be able to recall these bits of data at will, to see how they connect to one another, to be able to use them effectively in your own work—in other words, to understand this information.

What I'm encouraging, then, is that instructors design assignments that move students in general education courses beyond memorization and regurgitation in all its forms, toward application and deeper learning. After all, regardless of the type of curriculum or course we've developed (distributive, integrative, or somewhere in between), we want students to remember what they've learned so they can use it in their jobs and their daily lives. Furthermore, approaching assignment design this way lifts writing, oral communications, and quantitative reasoning above the level of basic skills that detract from the learning of content to a level that reflects what they really are: complex tools for critical thinking.

When designing assignments in either the insider-to-nonspecialist or the insider-to-public mode, it is important to remember the broader goals of the general education curriculum and the particular goals of your own course. Again, all assignments should be designed to ensure that students have learned the material you wish them to learn and can apply these materials in the ways you want them to.

An extended example may help to clarify this idea. I used to teach a first-year writing course that focused on the social functions of art—how, in other words, we use art individually and as a society. My goals for this class were as follows:

By the end of the course students should be able to

- Write an effective essay using the appropriate rhetorical methods given the particular audience and purpose
- Interpret individual responses to art
- Apply abstract concepts about art to particular works
- Analyze the role art plays in contemporary life

In the earliest iterations of this course, I assigned three papers:

1. Analyze a representational piece of art, pre-1850.
2. Analyze an abstract piece of art, post-1850.
3. Analyze the role art should play in society.

Certainly there's nothing wrong with these assignments. But after teaching the course once or twice and looking at the kinds of work I was receiving from students, I came to realize that I wasn't getting what I wanted from them. In the end, I had several issues with this series of assignments. First, there was a historical structure to them (and indeed, to the course as a whole) that wasn't necessary. Second, neither of the first two essays really explored the issue of art's function. Sure, students had to analyze the art, but to what end? Consequently, students weren't really prepared for the final essay, never having thought before about the roles art might play. Third, I found that the papers were written not just for me but to me. The first is inevitable: if it's an assigned paper, students may love it, but they're writing it because I made them. The second is not, and was undesirable in this context. Because students were writing to me, they were glossing terms, referencing class discussions as evidence, and generally riding on the fact that I knew the material better than they did. And in their reasoning at least, they felt they didn't need to explain it very carefully.

What I eventually came up with was a series of papers that followed my course goals very closely:

1. Analyze a piece of art that you like, using the formal elements to explain what emotional response it creates for you. Write to your classmates as a means of introducing yourself to them.

2. Use a quotation from our class readings to justify the necessity of abstract art in contemporary society. Write to a skeptical parent or guardian.

3. Make an argument justifying the use of university funds for the purchase of art, explaining the role that you think art should play in contemporary academia. Write to the university president.

Several things are worth noting here. First, each paper designates an audience. The first two might be considered public, while the third is more on the nonspecialist level. In each case, then, the rhetorical context forces the general education students to assume authority for their own knowledge and take on the responsibility of explaining the relevant concepts and ideas of the course to someone who isn't an enrollee. No glossing of terms here. No assumption of prior knowledge.

Second, the audiences change for each essay. In most occupations, employees have to write to a variety of readers: their coworkers, their managers, the CEO or board of trustees, clients, lawyers, suppliers, and the general public. Switching up the audiences of my assignments is my attempt to make students more aware of to whom they're writing and the ways in which different readers require different approaches. Parents, for example, will expect a more formal tone than friends, and the college president will require a tone even more formal still. In other words, creating different audiences creates writers with greater rhetorical flexibility.

Third, it's worth noting that the final paper for this course is a research paper. My sense was that students couldn't make the points they needed to the president solely through the use of logic and everyday examples; they needed to be able to cite outside sources that had a high degree of credibility. That said, the kinds of research a paper like this requires are rather different from the traditional approach of "choose a topic of your liking." Most notable perhaps, this paper pushes students to do research beyond the field of art. No one can answer a question about what role art should play in contemporary academia without looking at fields like sociology, politics, psychology, education, and philosophy. Therefore, the design of this assignment is highly integrative, pushing students to consider how these fields and others think about art—or how art might respond to the issues laid out by these fields.

Fourth, and arguably most important, these three assignments do a better job of giving me what I want: a greater sense of the degree to which students understand and can apply the concepts that drive my course. They can't do the first assignment—or indeed, any of them—if they don't know how to analyze the principles of design and the formal elements of art used to construct responses on the part of the audience (my first goal). The second paper clearly gets at my second goal: applying some of the theories that drive abstract art to a particular piece. And both of these essays better prepare students for the third paper, in which they must develop a theory about how art should operate in the social sphere.

Two additional points are worthy of mention here. First, the beginning and final assignments still allow a great deal of choice for the students: they can work with whatever artists, paintings, or sculptures they prefer. Although the second assignment allows students less choice—they must defend abstract art, whether or not they like it—they still have some flexibility when it comes to choosing a justification. And to the extent that this assignment forces writers to adopt a position they might oppose on a personal level—few of my students come into class loving abstract art—I would argue that assuming a position of intellectual objectivity is a crucial skill in academia, the workplace, and life in general.

And finally, these essays are more interesting for me to read. I never know what types of art students will choose for the first assignment—I've had everything from Rembrandt to Warhol to vampire goth to CD covers. Meanwhile, the second and third papers often bring into play discussions and events from fields I hadn't considered: eating disorders, gaming, social networks, chronic depression, string theory. While I won't claim that these papers are always more interesting to read—or that my reading pleasure should drive the course—let's face it: it doesn't hurt.

FURTHER EXAMPLES

This approach to assignment creation applies to more than just writing courses or writing-intensive courses. Here I note additional examples of how shifting audience and purpose can create assignments that more clearly assess student learning, push young scholars toward greater authority over course material, and engage them—and us—more productively. (While some of the following examples were developed over the course of my career in faculty development, many of them have evolved from samples in Barbara Tewksbury's excellent course design tutorial, The Cutting Edge. See Tewksbury and Macdonald, 2005.)

Insider to Nonspecialist

- *Biology:* ''You are on an environmental policy board that is looking into land reclamation in Victoria Harbor in Hong Kong. Your job is to explain to those on the board unfamiliar with the field of biology the impact of reclamation on marine life. As you do so, please keep in mind some of the key concepts we've discussed in the last few units, including but not limited to fecal coliform, species diversity, indicator species, and shore erosion.''

- *Literature:* ''You are on the board of a hospital deciding the curriculum for medical students in Wisconsin. Provide a rationale for the inclusion of a literature course in this curriculum, citing and analyzing three particular works from which you feel Wisconsin doctors would benefit.''

- *Art history:* ''Your department chair (in a field outside art) has asked you to explain why the study of art is necessary for someone in your major. Write an explanation, choosing at least three works of art to make your point. Be sure to analyze the art carefully, discussing the principles of composition and the elements of design.''

- *Education policy:* ''You are a member of the board of a private school considering expansion from primary education into secondary education. You've been through this process before and know the pros and cons and have been asked to explain them to the rest of the board. Once you've done this, make a recommendation, taking into consideration the key factors discussed in our lectures for this unit.''

Insider to Public

- *Physical education:* ''You have noticed on recent visits home that your aging parent seems to be gaining weight. Design an exercise regimen appropriate for his or her age, remembering our lessons on metabolism, bone density, diabetes, and other relevant factors.''

- *Mathematics:* "Write a letter to the editor of the *Columbus Dispatch* about the recent voting machine controversy. Explicitly use ratio and proportion to explain to the average reader why this topic bears further investigation."

- *Psychology:* "A friend comes to you asking for advice about a relationship in which one partner seems to be picking fights. The partner was emotionally abused as a child, and the friend wants to know how to keep the relationship going but end the dysfunction. Offer advice, applying at least three of the methods discussed in Chapter Six of the textbook."

- *Philosophy:* "You are now the caregiver for two teenage children of a friend who died. Which particular philosopher would you encourage these children to read? What corresponding literary work might you recommend? Explain your choices, referring to at least two of the scholarly articles we've discussed this term."

Although the audience and level of formality vary in the many of these examples, the quality of intellectual engagement does not. Students are expected to know the material and to be able to explain it to people who do not. In addition, these assignments ask for careful application of course methodologies—essentially, "Don't just show us that you know it; show us what you can *do* with it." Here again recall Zull's assertion that deeper, more lasting learning requires not just reflection but application. In using the information that we provide to them in our lectures and discussions and through the assigned texts, students increase the likelihood that they'll remember that information and be able to recall it later when it might be useful.

MATHEMATICS AND THE NATURAL SCIENCES

As may already be obvious, there's no reason that this approach can't be adapted to other kinds of student projects, including oral and poster presentations. There's no rule that says that students speaking to their classmates must address only that audience. Indeed, it makes a great deal more sense to require student speakers giving a talk on politics to speak to a hypothetical audience of politicians (perhaps state legislators). Similarly, it makes a lot more sense for students in a general education course on the sociology of violence to create a poster that speaks to an audience of high school boys rather than to a professor who already knows this stuff.

How, too, might a quantitative or scientific reasoning assignment be designed in a science or mathematics course that fulfills general education requirements? Often in my conversations with faculty from these disciplines, instructors express frustration that their students are able to do the problems, but they can't seem to explain the underlying concepts in written form. How might this change if a rhetorical context were created that not just expected but required a careful explanation in lay terms? A colleague of mine in chemistry asks her students to write about science "as though explaining it to English majors." She and I laugh when she says this, but we both know that it's an effective way to get students to process the information and learn it from the inside out rather than just reiterating the words of a text.

None of this equates to watered-down science—or at least no more watered down than is necessary (in any field) for a young adult approaching a complex topic for the first time. Consider, for instance, the following assignment from a biology course for nonmajors that focuses on food and culture (this is from Demystifying Foods: Why We Eat What We Eat, a course designed and taught by Marilee Ramesh at Roanoke College in May 2011):

> For your second group presentation, you get to do some role playing. You and your colleagues are a team working for the World Health Organization, evaluating the diets in specific regions of the world and presenting your findings as part of a public service announcement. You will pick your own teams for this assignment and will be randomly assigned a region of the world as the focus for your report.
>
> Your team will evaluate regional dietary habits using five case studies as specific examples. Consider these studies as interviews conducted in the field. Case studies will be selected from the book *What I Eat: Around the World in 80 Diets* [Menzel and D'Aluisio, 2010].
>
> Your presentation will be 20–25 minutes in length and should have visual aids (PowerPoint is recommended). This assignment is worth 15% of your course grade.
>
> In your presentation:
>
> a. Discuss the region you are evaluating. Provide some geographical and historical background for the area. Are there any major events that have recently occurred in the region?
>
> b. Who are the five individuals who you are using as examples?
>
> c. What types of food are people consuming? Consider the percentage of carbohydrates (sugars and starches), proteins (animal or plant), and fats in the diets. Are people eating whole foods or processed foods? Are they eating vegetables and fruits? You should be making generalizations for the region, not providing specific examples.
>
> d. Where are they getting their food? Hunting/gathering, farming, grocery, restaurant? How much of their diet is food they or someone in their family cooks, and how much is prepared elsewhere (processed or purchased food)? Is there a profession related to the food industry?
>
> e. Are they eating enough food or too much food? What is missing or overabundant in their diets? What influences their decisions on what they will eat that day? Do they have a healthy diet?
>
> f. Are there any external conditions that impact their diet or access to food? Consider economic, environmental, social, or cultural factors (think about wars, social unrest, droughts, etc.).

   g. Incorporate what you have discovered from the case studies with general statistics for your region. A place to start is pp. 330–331 of *What I Eat,* but you will want to find some additional sources. Do your specific case studies reflect a larger trend seen throughout the region?

   h. Propose your recommendations. What, if any, changes need to be made for the dietary conditions to be improved to result in a more nutritional diet for this region? Based on your understanding of nutrition, what recommendations does your group make, and how could these recommendations be implemented? Discuss both what should be done and how it could be set up.

Notable here is the degree to which students must know their science in order to succeed with this assignment: how to calculate carbohydrate, protein, and fat intake; the content of a healthy diet; and geographical influences on diet, for example. Notice as well that students aren't able to rely solely on what they've already read and learned from lectures; they'll have to collect more statistical data to show an understanding of their region. So research is required, but it's a specific, focused type of research that won't allow a data dump.

This is a highly integrated assignment. All science is of course connected to the world, but this assignment doesn't so much foreground those connections as bombard the student with them: this project can't occur in an acontextualized manner. And the assignment is also integrative in that it connects with so many of the fields from which the nonbiology enrollees in the course might come: politics, geography, sociology, chemistry, and so on.

In another example, Gary Hollis, a colleague of mine at Roanoke, teaches a general chemistry course for nonmajors focusing on the science of crime scene investigation (my impression is that these courses are popping up all over the country). One of the midterm assignments for the class has students analyze a poison. The prompt is as follows:

> Congratulations. You have been selected as one of seventeen finalists for the position of Crime Scene Investigator with the city of Las Vegas. The starting salary is $75,000, plus benefits. Ultimate success or failure in acquiring this job rests with your performance on the following test involving toxicological evidence.
> You will be evaluated on the report that you submit. This report should contain a brief description of the chemical and physical properties of your assigned toxin, an explanation of its origins (where it's found in nature, how it's isolated, etc.), a detailed description of its mode of action (how it works as a poison), and a longer section wherein you summarize the facts of a case in which this poison was used. As I evaluate your final reports, particular emphasis will be given to the following criteria:
>
>   1. Chemistry content (Is chemistry the focus of your paper? Is your chemistry content correct?)
>
>   2. Quality of research (Are your sources authoritative and credible? Have you cited appropriately?)

3. Paragraph structure (Does each paragraph have a topic sentence that is supported and illustrated by the details in the remaining sentences of that paragraph?)

4. Descriptive detail (Are your descriptions vivid and fresh without seeming stilted and clunky? Are your descriptions complete?)

5. Organization/clarity (Does your paper have a suitable introduction and conclusion? Are there appropriate transitions between sections? Is your prose clear?)

6. Format and standard usage (Does your report contain the required parts and follow the requested format? Will your report reflect positively on the department? Does it conform to accepted conventions of written English?)

This particular course is writing intensive by definition, which in part explains the last four criteria (although, of course, scientists care about these things too). Aside from that, what's being asked of the students is as real a form of science as occurs in most undergraduate science courses for nonmajors.

My sense is that nothing I'm saying here will shock those in the sciences: this is a discipline, after all, that has valued hands-on, contextualized learning in the form of required lab work almost since its conception. The suggestion that the applications of science and mathematics be made even more explicit, tying particular theories to real-world situations and uses, is not a radical shift.

Nevertheless, it's not uncommon in the general education context that our best intentions and best practices become watered down in ways that we hadn't anticipated. Courses that are shared among colleagues become no one's priority; textbooks become increasingly more standard and bland as publishers seek to increase their market share; a lack of lab space or lab assistants leads to a standardization of lab offerings in the name of efficiency. These trends are by no means limited to mathematics and the sciences, of course, and faced with them, we all tend to fall back on the way things have always been done and what we perceive to be safe and reliable.

Given all of this, sometimes it's good to shake things up a little. A case in point is a slightly quirkier example from a general education course on evolutionary biology. The first goal of the course states, ''Students will be able to describe and apply scientific methodologies appropriate for the course's discipline and topic.'' The course instructor, DorothyBelle Poli at Roanoke College who regularly publishes on alternative methods in the teaching of the sciences, provides students with the following assignment prompt:

Central dogma states that DNA is used to make RNA through transcription. RNA is then used to make protein through translation. These concepts are not always easy for students to grasp, and therefore, your mission will be to create a cartoon that depicts the process of *DNA → RNA → protein* in a way that would be helpful for another college student. You must use a metaphor for the process but make sure that you use appropriate scientific terms to help you explain the events. Make sure to label enzymes, proteins, etc. that we discussed in class. Cartoons should be taken seriously and should be drawn up to the best of your ability. You will be graded on creativity, professional presentation, and neatness alongside the accuracy of the scientific process. All *dogma cartoons will be collected and shown at a student-centered session titled* "Roanoke College Conference on Student Research & Creativity" held in the Colket Center on Saturday, March 19, 2011. *Please keep this in mind.*

This unorthodox assignment illustrates a number of valuable points:

- The idea that students are able to assume a greater degree of authority by pitching their work toward a less informed audience and that this sense of responsibility—of having to really know the material, not just make a nod in its direction—can lead to better, more detailed, deeper learning.

- The fact that different fields require different methods. Writing assignments work in a lot of fields, but not all of them, at least not all of the time. The sciences of course use writing, but often they favor a more efficient, lean approach that uses symbols, diagrams, and equations as well. In its own way, this assignment recognizes that need for efficiency and may better prepare students for other work in this field.

- This assignment involves an extremely complex cognitive challenge. On the face of it, this may seem like an overstatement—"It's just a picture!" some might mutter. "Worse: a *cartoon.*" But such a response misses the point: in order to create this cartoon, students must do *at least* all of the following:
  a. Understand a complex concept well enough to explain it to someone who hasn't taken the class.
  b. Be able to develop a metaphor, drawn from the world around them that relates to this concept.
  c. Turn that metaphor into a concrete image.
  This is no easy task, no mere reiteration "in your own words." Particularly noteworthy is the probability that because images are easier to recall than abstract ideas, having created a visual that explains this concept, students are more likely to remember it (Zull, 2002).

- This assignment has a greater authenticity than, say, a generic research paper and even many of the other assignments that I've described in this chapter. At the end of her prompt, the instructor for this course notes, "All dogma cartoons will be collected and shown at a student-centered session titled 'Roanoke College Conference on Student Research and Creativity' held in the Colket Center on Saturday, March 19, 2011." By adding this feature to the assignment, this professor has made real the fictitious audience of "another college student." This is no longer just an exercise:

real college students will see this! And your cartoon will either work or it won't.

Such an approach is miles beyond the old research assignment I discussed at the start of this chapter in which students pretend to be scholars in the field, adding their ideas to a scholarly conversation in which they can't possibly imagine themselves as real participants. For some of the best or most engaged students, that sort of pretend might be okay, but for many other students, the experience is highly dissociative and hardly seems like an approach that will spark lifelong interest in the topic or even in learning in general.

BREAKING THE MOLD

Finally, I chose to include the cartooning assignment because it makes the argument for thinking creatively when designing projects for students. I don't, of course, mean thinking creatively simply for the sake of being creative; there's too much at stake here for that sort of thing. Rather, my point is that we need to recognize that the demands of our particular courses—general education or otherwise—might require that we think beyond the sorts of writing, speaking, and quantification that we ourselves performed when we were students. In the end, traditional research papers may be irrelevant to many students today. Certainly some students will go on to graduate school and be grateful that they're able to scan vast amounts of information quickly and construct a cogent argument, and others will enter professions where similar skills are necessary from time to time. But for the vast majority of our graduates in the vast majority of their jobs? Not necessarily.

We need to create assignments where the methodology contributes to learning so that students have a greater chance of recalling, even years down the road, the information they encounter in our classes. Consider, for a moment, the writing class focusing on the functions of art that I described earlier in this chapter. What if, rather than having students write a single paper analyzing a piece of art that is meaningful to them, each student creates a blog in which she weekly analyzes works she's discovered? The instructor would give minimal, continual, nongraded feedback, and at the end of the course each student would revise what he considers to be his best three posts—really mini-essays—and hand in a portfolio that includes a cover essay explaining why he chose these three pieces and analyzing his own learning.

The effects of such an approach are vast. Not only is there a real audience for this assignment, creating greater authenticity for the student, but this audience is for digital media that will engage students as learners. Second, with this kind of assignment, students get repeated practice at the skill of careful analysis that is essential to this class, other classes, and life in general. Third, as they practice and practice, students are getting continual—as opposed to occasional—feedback on their efforts, something that research has repeatedly shown creates better learning (Ferren, 2010). Fourth, as the instructor provides this feedback, her role shifts from judge to coach. Our primary goal when we respond to less structured writing of this sort is not to evaluate students, but to urge them forward to better and better work. Fifth, because we don't feel pressure to justify a grade, these responses become easier to write, less formal, and more dialogic. Finally, this kind of feedback requires students to assume greater authority over their work. We're guiding and coaching them, but they make the decision about what direction to take as they revise their pieces.

That they must be able to rationalize their final choices for the portfolio is a bonus. This is essentially a metacognitive act, requiring students to think about their own thinking and learning. As Peggy Maki states so eloquently, this kind of self-reflection "reinforces learning by engaging learners in focused thinking about their understanding and misunderstanding" (2010, p. 48).

Just because this project uses a medium with which students are comfortable and is pitched to a less informed audience does not mean that lower standards are applied in creating the work or in grading it. University students should be held to the highest intellectual standards possible, regardless of the rhetorical context of the assignment. Indeed, one study, from the Wabash College Center for Inquiry in the Liberal Arts (2007), has found that "academic challenge and high expectations" is one of the key components for successful student learning.

Consider some of the other possibilities. Might we not require students to design a Web site educating a particular population—say, premenopausal women—about healthy eating habits? Or might we not require students to write a minidrama that explains string theory to high school students? Or create a podcast that enacts an ethical question taught in a general education philosophy course? At the very least, why not ask students in an education or a psychology course to write a dialogue between Lev Vygotsky and Jean Piaget, analyzing the impact of technology on the development of adolescents? All of these assignments are integrative in nature, connecting what happens in the classroom to what matters in the world. And all of them have the potential to light up the classroom, engaging students more deeply in their learning, and creating the kinds of intellectual mind-sets that lead to lifelong learning and lifelong learners.

CHAPTER SIX

The Chapter You May Want to Skip

Institutional Assessment and General Education

I was at a faculty meeting on campus a few years back when our head of assessment, a biologist who is well liked and has a good head on his shoulders, got up to talk about the current state of institutional assessment on our campus. We'd just completed a successful reaccreditation process with the Southern Association of Schools and Colleges, our regional organization, and Tom was basically there to remind us that now was the time to build on our positive review and take steps to continue a productive assessment routine for the coming years. As he made several salient points, his colleagues listened politely, nodding here and there or asking for clarification when they were confused. Then Tom concluded his remarks. "Any questions?"

A hand went up.

"Yes?"

The questioner, a senior faculty member, paused for a moment, trying to find the right words. "Tom ...," he said.

"Uh-huh?"

"When you're writing about assessment ..."

"Yes?"

"And you're taking notes—how do you abbreviate it? Assessment, I mean."

ASSESSMENT THAT LACKS INTEGRITY

At the risk of generalizing, this pretty much sums up most faculty members' view of assessment:

- It's a pain in the ... well, butt.
- It's busywork.
- It's busywork to please some higher-ups somewhere, who are themselves intent on pleasing an outside organization wielding a rather large bully stick.
- It's baloney.
- It's not really what we're about.

And fair enough. The first few times I encountered assessment, it went something like this:

1. Somewhere, long long ago before I was hired, some committee made up of people who were now retired met in a dark room and decided a bunch of "learning outcomes" for the general education program.

2. At the end of every academic year, everyone else teaching in general education would receive an e-mail from the director of the program that read something along the following lines: "This year we'll be assessing learning outcome 2.165: 'Students will be familiar with key works of art and literature from Western civilization.' Once you have determined your students' final grades for the semester, please send me an e-mail letting me know what percentage of your students received a C or better on their oral presentations involving key works of art or literature from Western civilization."

3. I would delete this e-mail.

4. Or sometimes I wouldn't. Sometimes I would be a good citizen, dutifully opening my notebook once all the grades were determined and counting the number of students who'd received at least a C. Then I'd get out my calculator, figure out the percentage, and send that number to my director.

5. Later I would learn that the response rate to the director's e-mail was somewhere in the low fortieth percentile.

I should say right off the bat that I don't blame any of the various general education program directors I served under for this approach. It's the same process that pretty much every program and major on campus followed. Indeed, when I became the director of general education, it's the approach that I used.

That said, there's a lot wrong here, much of which helps to explain faculty attitudes toward assessment. For one thing, this approach to assessment is an add-on: it's additional work, above and beyond what we already do. Granted, the work isn't that difficult, but that makes it almost worse: this feels like stupid work, busywork. Related to this, this task seems to have little value in comparison to the real work we're doing—our teaching, our research. We count the grades, we do the calculations, we send them along, and we never see them again—as if we needed any more evidence that these numbers don't matter.

And above and beyond the sheer fussiness of this assessment model lies something else: what I'm being asked to assess, the outcome I'm doing the number crunching for, seems lame. Although I want my students to be "familiar" with the best works of Western civilization, somehow that word doesn't quite capture what I'm after. I didn't get into this field to create "familiarity" on the part of my students. They can get familiarity with works of art and literature by going to a museum, reading a book or magazine, or surfing the Net. A monkey could become familiar with art just by looking at a statue at the zoo.

I spent seven years in graduate school, battled through a tough job market, and over the past fifteen years of my life have divided my evenings between grading papers, prepping for class, and doing my own research and writing because I think art and literature matter: I think they change lives. It's not familiarity I'm after, but engagement—the sort of emotional and intellectual curiosity that leads a student to continue exploring my subject long after the grade has been posted, long after the campus bookstore has stopped its buy-backs. And I'm guessing most faculty, from most fields, feel the same way about their work.

Part of the problem, then, is that assessment often doesn't seem to assess the things that faculty care about. A variation on this is a comment I've heard a lot when talking to faculty about assessment: "What I do can't be quantified," or, "If you can measure it, it's not what I care about." Put another way, faculty often feel that what they do in the classroom—the changes they evoke in students—is intangible. Certainly I understand this point of view. The best moments for me when teaching are when a student asks a question I hadn't anticipated, or makes an observation I'd never thought about, or shows up at my office after class wondering if perhaps we could do an independent study on some item or issue or text from the course that grabbed her curiosity. These things are hard to weigh, measure, and count. And I'm guessing I'm not alone in taking pleasure in these moments.

All of this likely feeds from and plays into our belief that assessment is administrative folly—busywork dreamed up at some conference somewhere. The administration tells us we need assessment and tells us what to assess, and we give them meaningless numbers to keep them (and the accreditation agencies) happy.

In essence, assessment as it's often practiced tends to lack integrity. I use this term in both its more connotative, ethical sense—"He's a politician who lacks integrity"—and its broader, more concrete sense: "This building lacks integrity." Often when I'm discussing assessment with others, I find myself thinking about the Eiffel Tower, about its grace and beauty and structural integrity. And I'm struck by two thoughts:

- The Eiffel Tower could not be built from the top down.
- The Eiffel Tower could not be built out of paper.

I suppose that in a literal sense, both of these statements may be incorrect, but I will nevertheless run with my analogy in order to make what I consider to be two key points about assessment:

1. As long as the components of assessment and its protocols are determined at the top of an institution's academic structure, faculty will likely be dissatisfied with assessment for all of the reasons mentioned above.

2. As long as the raison d'être for an institution's assessment is to create a paper trail to please the accreditation and assessment gods, assessment will likely continue to be a bane to faculty existence.

CREATING ASSESSMENT WITH INTEGRITY

How, then, do we create assessment that has integrity, particularly in a general education program, an area that at most institutions constitutes a faculty member's secondary teaching assignment?

A few ideas come to mind:

The determination of what is to be assessed should be dialogic.

Generally assessment is viewed as the verification that institutional goals are being met, so there is the assumption of an alignment from the very top of the institution to the very bottom (Figure 6.1). In Figure 6.1, everything that occurs at the course level is determined at the institutional level: institutional learning objectives are determined by institutional mission, program objectives (whether in general education or in the major) are determined by the institutional objectives, and the course learning outcomes are determined by the program's stated goals.

In practical terms, this means that when assessment time comes around, the people doing the assessing are seldom the ones who have decided what to

Figure 6.1. Top-Down Assessment

examine. Consequently, even if the final data are shared with everyone, it's less likely that faculty will pay attention because these matters may not reflect their concerns at all.

A more productive approach would ensure that the street-level instructors—the ones in the classroom who work with the students—are involved in selecting what is to be assessed. Are they concerned that their students aren't learning how to analyze texts effectively? Are they wondering if there's a better way to teach students to write lab reports? Is there a worry that students aren't finding ways to apply course material to real-life situations? If these are the issues keeping instructors awake at night, then that is what should be examined.

Of course, such an approach isn't always feasible. On occasion there are outcomes that the institution hasn't assessed for a while and for which they must gather data. And on occasion there are broader, more institution-wide matters that need to be examined. But at moments like these, faculty at the course level should at least be consulted about the process and the particulars. If they are to be engaged in the process, they must feel that their voices, their concerns, and the trends they see with their students are addressed. In the end, it's not a matter of reversing the arrows in Figure 6.1 so that they are going upward, the courses and programs driving the mission, but of creating a dialogue that involves all of the shareholders at a school, wherein concerns are met at all levels and agency is granted to everyone involved. When it's time to decide what is to be assessed this year, the e-mails should be going back and forth, not coming down from on high.

Assessment works best when it focuses on quality enhancement as opposed to (just) quality assurance.

Put another way, assessment should do something, lead to something, particularly something that allows a general education program to evolve in constructive ways (Gaston, 2010b; Walvoord, 2010). The purpose of assessment in general education should be to tell faculty what is working and what is not, and how things might be improved. Peggy Maki (2010) states it thus: "Determining that 75 percent of the students have satisfactorily demonstrated a general education outcome represents a commitment to *accountability*. But a commitment to identifying patterns of strength and weakness in that 75 percent, as well as in the remaining 25 percent, and to discovering the reasons for those patterns represents openness to learn more about the teaching/learning process and ways to improve it" (p. 49, my emphasis).

In other words, feeding the administration the numbers they want and need is unsatisfying. It proves we're doing our jobs at a satisfactory level, but we already knew that—and knowing that doesn't necessarily help us do our jobs better.

Rather than envisioning the uses of assessment as a line moving upward, with faculty at the bottom level passing data to the administration at the top level, it's more productive to think of it as a circle (Figure 6.2). As may already be obvious, step 4 returns to step 1, and the cycle repeats. Once a new approach has been developed based on the perceived strengths and weaknesses, then new data are collected, reexamined, and so on. What's key here is that the assessment process generates usable data that will help us improve our programs, teaching, and student learning. In this way, the assessment process becomes less alienating and less of a waste of time: it creates information that is useful to us as scholars and teachers.

Of course, some who look at this diagram may gasp in dismay and think, "That's too much work! I'd rather just count the grades in my book and send an e-mail!" This is a perfectly understandable reaction and leads to my next point.

As much as possible, assessment should be aligned with the work that faculty and students already do.

This idea first hit home with me when I spent a year working at an educational institution in Hong Kong. I kept hearing people talk about "student assessments." I assumed at first that they meant institutional assessment at the student level, which, of course, is always where it should be (Maki, 2010). What I eventually realized is that my Hong Kong, Chinese, British, Australian, New Zealand, and Canadian colleagues were using the terms *assessment* and *assignment* synonymously—that in British parlance, *assessment* is the word for describing the kinds of work one has students turn in for evaluation.

This is a key concept: whenever possible, the data we're gathering for the purposes of Assessment with a capital A—that is, Assessment to keep the administration happy—should come from the work we're already having students do. In other words, rather than creating new activities that add to our workload and cut into class time, we should use the assignments we're already having students do.

This is something of a double-edged sword, I will admit. On the one hand, it very clearly addresses some of the workload issues mentioned above: faculty won't have to add assignments to their courses and won't have additional evaluating to do. On the other hand, as Figure 6.2 makes clear with its mention of "embedded" assessments, this can mean that a faculty member might have to shift out an assignment or assessment she ordinarily uses and replace it with one designed by a collaborative of faculty and administrators that's decided a particular outcome needs to be examined. Regardless, there's no additional work, simply different work.

One bonus of this approach is that it is likely to lead to more accurate data regarding student learning. Because the assessment tool is part of the syllabus, there's a greater likelihood that class lectures, discussions, readings, and so on

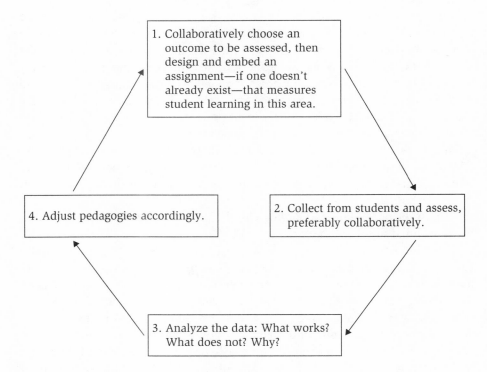

Figure 6.2. Assessment for Quality Enhancement

will be aimed at preparing students for this assessment. To put it another way, students shouldn't be hit with an assessment out of the blue. Another bonus is that when assessment data are derived from assignments that are already part of the class, it's generally an indication that the outcome being assessed is closely related to faculty concerns about the course. Because the data are being drawn from assignments we've created on our own or collaboratively with colleagues, there's likely greater intrinsic motivation on our part, meaning greater engagement. As a result, assessment ceases to be an alienating process, performed simply to please administrators.

In addition, this concept expands beyond in-class assignments. There are any number of opportunities to overlap assessment with our "real" work. At a basic level, for instance, assessment links naturally with pedagogical development for faculty. In the midst of the assessment cycle, those in charge of faculty development should be paying attention to the trends emerging from the data. What sorts of workshops might emerge naturally out of what we're already doing? Perhaps a session or two on designing more effective assignment and project prompts or one on integrating research methods in a more effective way? These are the kinds of workshops that teaching and learning centers run anyway, but linking them to assessment data both gives them a sense of immediate worth they might otherwise lack and reinforces the sense that assessment serves a purpose above and beyond holding off the accreditation hounds, helping to improve our teaching and our programs and our students' learning.

Consider the first-year-seminar (FYS) portfolio at Coe College in Cedar Rapids, Iowa. Two weeks before the end of their first term, students hand in a collection of what they consider to be their best writing from the term, for which they receive a final portfolio grade from their instructor. The portfolio is then scored for assessment purposes by two faculty other than the student's FYS instructor: an instructor familiar with the course content in this FYS section and a faculty member teaching another FYS section. The two faculty members provide a holistic evaluation of the portfolio on a six-point scale and a written commentary on the portfolio. Students thus receive two scores and two sets of comments. If the two faculty scores do not agree, a third reader, typically someone from the Rhetoric Department, will weigh in with a third assessment. The FYS instructor does not do an assessment scoring. One advantage of this system, according to Bob Marrs, coordinator of Coe's writing across the curriculum program, is that the system essentially achieves multiple ends. For one thing, the portfolios create multiple levels of assessment: students are involved in self-assessment because every portfolio requires a preface with commentary on writing process, discussing how these papers interconnect and comparing these compositions with previous work; second, FYS faculty can compare their assessment of the students' work with how outside readers assess those same texts; and, third, the FYS portfolios provide the college with a means for understanding how well students are doing at the end of their first term in college and then serve as a basis for various program assessment projects.

Finally, the process is a form of faculty development. Because faculty are reading papers from other courses and discussing these papers and the assignments that prompted them with other faculty from other fields, there's an exchange of pedagogical techniques that enriches the vocabulary and practice of all who participate. Indeed, given this, it would be smart, as Linda Suskie (2009) recommends, to involve as many faculty as possible in general education assessment, including adjuncts. Doing so helps to create a more transparent, cohesive, and productive professional environment.

Granted, this approach is more complicated than having each professor sit alone in her office and grade the papers from her class. But any time you can kill three birds with one stone—well, that's not just efficient: that's smart.

We need to assess what really matters to us.

Paul Gaston (2010a) puts it this way: "Properly conceived and implemented, assessment provides a productive focus on overriding questions of priority" (p. 14). It's incumbent on faculty at the program and course level to design outcomes that address the matters that really concern them. Part of the problem with assessing student familiarity with "key works of art and literature" is that it doesn't reflect my highest aspirations for the general education classroom. When I'm standing in front of a room full of mathematicians and scientists enrolled in my Artistic and Literary Responses to Science and Technology course, I want more than familiarity from my students. I want them to care about literature, to recognize that it matters, that it can very literally save lives. As corny as this sounds, my conversations with faculty from across the disciplines assure me that they share similar feelings about their own fields and their own teachings: they want students to understand that the course material is relevant to living informed, productive lives.

If that's the case, we need to ensure that the assessment process addresses this. It won't be easy. I can't just ask my pupils, "Do you care about literature?" Any student with half a clue, asked such a question by a starry-eyed professor holding a grade book, will of course answer, "Yes." In many ways, this parallels the "What I do can't be quantified" conundrum: How do we ensure that assessment takes into consideration not just what can be counted but our highest ambitions for the classroom?

I answer this question with a simple maxim: we should aim as high as possible, as close as we can come to our ideals, while remaining measurable. The first part of this equation is easy enough: if what we care about is, say, students appreciating the concept of scientific objectivity or students recognizing the way in which poetry lifts the reader out of a soul-crushing materiality, then that's what we need to assess. The second part of this statement makes it clear, though, that we might not be able to assess these matters in their purest form. For instance, instead of asking students, "Do you appreciate the scientific method?" ("Yes!"), we might create an assessment project that asks them to design an experiment employing the scientific method for their majors and exploring the benefits of such an approach for the greater population. Or we might ask a student in the general education literature classroom to write an essay addressed to a family member, recommending a single poem that they feel might be important to this person's life.

Such an approach doesn't guarantee that students will fall in love with scientific objectivity, poetry, or any other subject matter. But because it asks students to invest in a way of thinking about the world that they wouldn't otherwise consider, I believe that this approach increases the probability that these perspectives will become ingrained into their worldview.

In essence, all of this is just another way of encouraging faculty to not give up on their ideals when asked to do assessment and to be creative. Everything is assessable to a point. If you want to provide evidence that your students are discussing the course material with increasing levels of complexity, spot-check threaded online discussions based on a prompt of your choosing. Or if you want students to adopt Native American philosophies, ask them to design a life plan engaging these ideas.

These approaches may not hit exactly what we're after, but assessing these assignments will give us a sense of how close students are to reaching our goals and will provide us valuable information to help us improve the teaching of our general education classes, which is the real purpose of assessing anything. That these methods would also provide us with numbers to keep the administration happy is simply a bonus.

Assessment should be written into a general education program from the start.

If we're going to make assessment meaningful to and easier for general education faculty, we need to be deliberate about writing it into the structure of the program. An assessment protocol that is added at the last minute or is layered artificially over the top of an existing program will probably feel like extra work. A protocol that is woven into the program and is an inextricable part of the whole, however, isn't extra: it's what we do.

The concept of e-portfolios provides a good example. The bare-bones outline of the portfolio system is relatively easy to understand:

- Individual students have an electronic portfolio, very much like a Web site, to which they add artifacts—papers, presentations, lab reports, and so on—on an annual or biannual basis. These artifacts should include work from their general education classes, but might also include work from their major courses. Indeed, including both would likely lead to greater integration of general education and the major, to the benefit of both. Students maintain these portfolios throughout their time at the university.

- The best portfolio systems also require students to include metacognitive essays in which they synthesize their experiences over the course of a term or terms. What connections do they see among the artifacts they've submitted? What differences? What skills do they think they can carry over from their general education courses to their major? What skills in their major have helped them succeed in general education? How have they grown as learners? What obstacles have they faced? How might their educational goals or plans for the future have changed?

- These portfolios are generally administered by the university information technology office, and sample portfolios can be extracted from across a number of variable sets for assessment or other purposes. For example, if the year's assessment tasks require an examination of a sophomore-level humanities course, a random sampling can be pulled from the second year and examined. Similarly, if faculty need to perform a longitudinal study of students over years at university, appropriate files can be made available.

The key to the portfolio system is that it's good pedagogy. Meta-analysis of this sort helps students come to understand themselves as learners: what their skills are, how they need to improve, what techniques have led them to successful work (Suskie, 2009). Moreover, analyzing how different fields within a general education curriculum and between general education and their own majors will help them develop a flexibility of mind that will be invaluable in the workplace and in a complex and ever-changing world. We don't just want students to encounter different fields and different methodologies; we want them to be deliberative about how the thinking in one field might help them in another. What problems are they facing now? How do these new problems compare to challenges they've encountered in the past? What intellectual skill helped them overcome these obstacles in the past? How might these methods be adapted to current matters?

E-portfolios are good teaching: they allow students the opportunity to develop problem-solving skills that will prepare them for the challenges of productive citizenship and successful employment. This alone makes including a portfolio system an appealing option as an institution revises its general education curriculum.

But e-portfolios also make assessment easier, giving faculty and administrators access to a wide range of student work and data: from individual classes, from campuswide courses, from particular levels of students, from a longitudinal cross-section. Without this kind of portfolio requirement in place in the general education program, gathering these kinds of data is cumbersome for both the administration and the faculty. Nobody wants that.

My point is not that every school needs to have an e-portfolio system. As I stated when I began this book, every institution needs to develop its own approach to general education—one that reflects its culture, the unique needs of its students, and the character of its faculty.

In the end, the key idea is that assessment works better if, as a school develops a new general education program or refines its old program, thought is given to how assessment might become an intrinsic part of what we do. It blends seamlessly into our pedagogies, the work of our students, and all the other things that drive us when we're in the classroom—and indeed, something that helps us do these things better. Because only when assessment is less of an add-on and more of a tool for successful student learning will it cease to be a pain in the ... well, you know what.

CONCLUSION

When all is said and done, general education is perhaps best described as both a responsibility and an opportunity. We have a responsibility to prepare our students for the challenges of work and global citizenship outside the academy. This means providing them with the knowledge and methodologies and skills of our fields, but also with the intellectual flexibility that will allow them to adapt thoughtfully and productively to the rapid changes of the workplace—and, indeed, the changes taking place in the world at large.

I once heard a department chair make the distinction between "line workers" and "line managers." He was speaking both literally and figuratively, making the point that we hope our students will leave the university capable of being at the top of the management ladder rather than at the bottom.

But perhaps this isn't all we should strive for. Perhaps, in today's complex world, there's some third option that involves creating graduates who don't just assume the position that's assigned to them or work their way to the top of the heap. Perhaps we're really after graduates who are able to look at a situation and offer an alternative to the existing paradigm, questioning the need for a ladder, for a heap, for a multitiered system of managers and line workers.

Creating this sort of graduate is a complicated proposition and can be challenging, changing the dynamic of the classroom, forcing us to reconsider our approach to teaching and to our students in general, indeed, raising issues about the very timbre of our profession. And all of this is a great responsibility.

That this responsibility does not translate into an easy task is perhaps a deterrent for some. We are busy, after all, feeling pressure from multiple forces that drive our work. But for others, this lack of ease may provide some comfort: this is hard work, yes, but at least it's not busywork, and it's not brainless. Revising a core curriculum, redesigning courses and assignments, and assessing a program in productive ways so that students can move forward into the world as productive members of a fast-changing society is intellectual work, requiring the same kinds of focus and concentration that we apply in our labs, our research, and our teaching. And, engaged in this way, these curricular revisions can provide us with some of the same rewards as does our other work: a sense of accomplishment, increased insights, increased intellectual curiosity, and stronger relationships with colleagues. As a result, the decision of a campus to tackle a curricular revision can be viewed as an opportunity.

It's an opportunity in other ways as well. When we're asked to whittle time out of our cramped schedules and be deliberate about how we're teaching a general education course—to think carefully about our audience and the goals for that audience—more often than not, we find approaches to the classroom that we'd previously overlooked. We might, for example, see an opportunity to teach a topic that is normally not addressed in our tightly structured majors: sky diving, for instance, or pre-Raphaelite art, or Quaker philosophy, or gun laws. While our Puritan heritage seems to insist that pleasure—for the professor or the students—shouldn't be a primary goal of the university classroom, certainly we are better at our work, more invested, more willing to take intellectual risks when we are more emotionally engaged.

I have a friend, a brilliant scholar, teacher, and administrator named Eugene Eoyang, who had a long and illustrious career at the University of Indiana before spending a decade in Hong Kong working with the general education program at Lingnan University. He liked to argue that most of the important discoveries of recent decades came from crossing boundaries, "from putting together unlike things and seeing what happened. Nothing new comes from looking at the same old, same old." General education, he would say, gives instructors the chance to try new methods and explore how things connect.

All of us believe our fields matter. All of us believe that understanding physics or philosophy, sociology or chemistry, literature or psychology makes better citizens, better employees (and employers), better human beings. Having studied these topics allows our students to interact with the world in more informed and productive ways. General education allows us to take that message to students we wouldn't always have contact with otherwise. And it gives us the chance to enjoy ourselves as we do so.

Syllabus for Artistic and Literary Responses to Science and Technology

INQ 261

Artistic and Literary Responses to Science and Technology

Professor Paul Hanstedt

Miller 222

375–2380 (office)

(540) 464–6299 (home; call long distance direct and I'll call you back)

e-mail: hanstedt@roanoke.edu

Office hours: Mondays, 12:30–3:00; Tues. and Thurs., 2:45–4:00; and by appointment

Course Goals

This course takes a theme-based approach to Humanities II, examining literary and artistic responses to science, scientific methodology, and technology. The syllabus is designed in such a way that by the end of the course, each student will be able to

- Analyze the details of a poem, novel, or painting in order to construct a cogent reading of the piece.

- Assess the ramifications—both positive and negative—of industry and technology on individuals and society using course readings, discussions, and research as a foundation.
- Analyze the relationship between technology/industry—as portrayed in literature and art—and their own lives.

Texts

Dick, Philip K. *Do Androids Dream of Electric Sheep?* New York: Ballantine Books, 1968.

Dickens, Charles. *Hard Times.* New York: Signet Classics, 2008.

English Romantic Poetry. Ed. Stanley Appelbaum. Mineola, N.Y.: Dover Publications, 1996.

English Victorian Poetry. Ed. Paul Negri. Mineola, N.Y.: Dover Publications, 1999.

Hemingway, Ernest. *The Sun Also Rises.* New York: Scribner, 1926.

Shelley, Mary. *Frankenstein.* New York: Penguin Classics, 2003.

Strickland, Carol. *The Annotated Mona Lisa.* Kansas City: Andrews and McMeel, 1992.

Assignments

There are three major components to the work in this class. The first is a series of group projects where you and four classmates explore the day's reading (see the syllabus), writing a mini-essay that asks and attempts to answer a question of your choosing that you feel leads to insights about the material at hand.

The second assignment asks you and a partner to research a particular painter of the late eighteenth, nineteenth, or twentieth century and to present a painting by that artist to the class, with some explanation of the work, its reflection of the period out of which it came, and its significance to our discussions about industry and technology. Be sure to pay attention to the formal elements of art as you construct your argument.

Your final project asks you to answer this question: Finally, what are the consequences of technology on the human soul? Carefully analyze two of the works we've encountered this semester to see how the writers/painters answer this question. Do you agree? Explain why. Feel free to draw upon your major or a field you're interested in pursuing.

In addition to formal papers, students will be asked to write a single-spaced, one-page exploratory response to readings at least once a week. These jottings are a form of prewriting, a chance for you to develop, in an informal way, some of the ideas you'll tackle in your major papers. At least once a week, I want you to choose a quotation from the reading that interests you, confuses you, or challenges you. Then unpack the quote, explaining what you see happening in it, why it interests you. If it's a quotation that confuses you, spend some time attempting to unravel it. In order to receive an A for this portion of your grade, you will need to turn in and receive a check mark on 90% of these jottings; 80–89% will earn you a B; and 70–79% will earn you a C. Less than 70% and you'll have to take the class over.

Late papers or presentations will be downgraded one-third of a grade for each day they are late. Failure to turn in a paper within a week of the due date or a draft of a paper before the next draft is due or to participate in a presentation will lead to an F in the course. Problems with computers, printers, automobiles, jobs, cats, dogs, or roommates will not be accepted as valid excuses.

Course Requirements

Daily responses	10%
Painting presentation	10%
Group papers	15% (5% each)
Consequences essay	30%
Final exam	25%
Quizzes & participation	10%

Attendance

Because learning is a collaborative process, attendance for this course is required. More than two absences will result in the final grade for the course being lowered by one-third of a grade for each additional absence. If excessive absences (more than four) occur, a student will be dropped from the roster. (Excessive tardiness can lead to students being marked absent.)

If you do miss class for some reason, be certain to contact someone to make sure you understand what occurred in class that day and what is due for the next class. *If you miss class on a day when work is due, you MUST provide written evidence of illness in order to receive full credit for that day's work.*

PLEASE NOTE: There are two days, Tuesday 14 and Thursday 16 April, where attendance is absolutely mandatory. No excuse, short of the death of an immediate family member, will be accepted for missing on these days. A failure to attend on those days will, at the least, lead to a lowering of your major paper grade and could lead to an F in the course.

A Few Notes Regarding Classroom Etiquette

- You must bring *all* textbooks relevant to each day's reading to class. This is so that we can examine readings in detail and so that you can remember those details on the final exam. A repeated failure to bring relevant works will be seen as a sign of disengagement with the course, and could lead to a student being marked absent for the day, or to dismissal from the course.

- Cell phones and related electronic instruments are distracting and disrespectful. Keep them off and put them away, or you may find yourself buying a new one. No exceptions.

A Word About the Syllabus

You'll notice that this syllabus is a little different from what you may have seen in your Humanities I course. For one thing, it moves backward, beginning with the questions and the literatures that will be most familiar to us and moving toward more historically situated—if not more complicated—conversations from the past. Second, our discussions will be organized around three "case studies," major works that by themselves capture some of the essential questions for the eras we are examining. Surrounding each of these works are smaller—though not less significant—readings that can help us understand the context out of which each of our case studies arose. Simultaneously, of course, our major works may serve to illuminate the poems and paintings that provide context.

SYLLABUS

Case Study #1: *Do Androids Dream of Electric Sheep?*

Tuesday, 13 January
Course introduction; the formal elements of art

Thursday, 15 January

Do Androids Dream of Electric Sheep? 3–68
Mona Lisa, 170–171, 177

Tuesday, 20 January

Do Androids Dream of Electric Sheep? 69–154
Mona Lisa, 145, 174–176

Thursday, 22 January

Do Androids Dream of Electric Sheep? 154–202
FIRST GROUP PROJECT DUE: 1 typewritten question relevant to the day's reading

Tuesday, 27 January

Do Androids Dream of Electric Sheep? 203–244

Handout: Heidegger, ''Modern Science, Metaphysics, and Mathematics''

The Sun Also Rises, 1–47

DUE: First group paper, in the mailbox outside my office, no later than noon

Thursday, 29 January

The Sun Also Rises, 48–108

Mona Lisa, 148–151, 158–161

Tuesday, 3 February

The Sun Also Rises, 108–191

Handout: A sociological perspective on technology

Thursday, 5 February

The Sun Also Rises, 192–250

Handout: Selected modernist poetry

Handout: Heidegger, ''The Question Concerning Technology''

Case Study #2: *Hard Times*

Tuesday, 10 February

Hard Times, 9–94

Mona Lisa, 83–86, 89–90, 92–95

Thursday, 12 February

English Victorian Poetry:
    Arnold: ''Dover Beach,'' 114; ''The Buried Life,'' 120
    C. Rossetti: ''An Apple Gathering,'' 156; '' 'No, Thank You, John,' '' 158

Handout: Elizabeth Barrett Browning: ''The Cry of the Children''

Mona Lisa, 80

Tuesday, 17 February

Hard Times, 94–182

SECOND GROUP PROJECT DUE: 1 type-written question relevant to the day's reading

Thursday, 19 February

English Victorian Poetry:
　　R. Browning: "My Last Duchess," 49; "Prophyria's Lover," 53
　　D. G. Rossetti: "The Blessed Damozel," 142; "The Choice," 146

Monday, 23 February

　　DUE: Second group paper, in the mailbox outside my office, no later than noon

Tuesday, 24 February

　　Hard Times, 183–231

　　Mona Lisa, 96, 99–105

Thursday, 26 February

　　First round of painting presentations

SPRING BREAK!

Tuesday, 10 March

　　Hard Times, 231–300

　　English Victorian Poetry:
　　　　Tennyson: "The Lady of Shalott," 4
　　　　Morris: "Shameful Death," 175

　　Mona Lisa, 112, 114–119

Thursday, 12 March

　　NO CLASS!!!!

Case Study #3: *Frankenstein*

Tuesday, 17 March

　　English Romantic Poetry:
　　　　Wordsworth: "The World Is Too Much with Us," 51

　　Frankenstein, 6–52
　　Mona Lisa, 76–82

Thursday, 19 March

　　English Romantic Poetry:
　　　　Wordsworth: "Lines Composed a Few Miles Above Tintern Abbey," 25;
　　　　　　"London, 1802," 41

Mona Lisa, 68–70; 72–73

Tuesday, 24 March

English Romantic Poetry:
  Wordsworth: "The Solitary Reaper," 41; "My Heart Leaps Up," 33; "Nutting," 29
  Coleridge: "Frost at Midnight," 100; "This Lime-Tree Bower My Prison," 60

THIRD GROUP PROJECT DUE: 1 typewritten question relevant to the day's reading

Thursday, 26 March

Frankenstein, 52–111

Handout: Coleridge, "The Eolian Harp"

Friday, 27 March

DUE: Third group paper, e-mailed to me no later than noon

Tuesday, 31 March

Frankenstein, 111–162

English Romantic Poetry:
  Coleridge: "Kubla Khan," 105

Wednesday, 1 April

DUE: Complete draft of final essay, in my office, no later than noon

Thursday, 2 April

English Romantic Poetry:
  Coleridge: "The Rime of the Ancient Mariner," 63
  Shelley: "Ozymandias," 147; "The Waning Moon," 162

Tuesday, 7 April

Frankenstein, 162–221

English Romantic Poetry:
  Keats: "Ode to a Nightingale," 216

Thursday, 9 April

Second round of painting presentations

Tuesday, 14 April

DUE: Polished draft of final paper (4 copies; no late or incomplete papers allowed)

Thursday, 16 April

Peer responding: **Attendance absolutely mandatory**

Monday, 20 April

DUE: Final draft of final paper, in my mailbox no later than noon

Friday, 24 April

Final exam, 2:00–5:00

Syllabus for The Way Things Work: Sky Diving and Deep Sea Diving

INQ 250—Scientific Reasoning I: The Way Things Work: Sky Diving and Deep Sea Diving

Fall 2011: 12:00–2:10 p.m.

Instructor: Mrs. Bonnie W. Price

Office: Trexler 161B

Office phone: 540–375–2408

E-mail: price@roanoke.edu

Office hours: MWF: 10:00 a.m. – 12:00 noon; Tuesday/Thursday: by appointment

Required Materials

Text: Explorations in Physics; Jackson, Laws & Franklin; Wiley & Sons, Inc., 2003

Supplies: 1-inch binder used only for this course containing individual sheets of graph paper either purchased or printed from http://incompetech .com/graphpaper/, writing instrument(s), small ruler, basic calculator that is not on a phone or computer, and *A Writer's Reference* by Diana Hacker.

Course Content Description and Teaching Methods

This scientific reasoning course is based on the theme of sky diving and deep sea diving, designed to address the fundamental questions, "Why study motion, and what factors contribute to the motion of an object?" The basic laws of physics applicable to motion will be investigated through experimentation. Very little formal lecturing will take place; instead, the class will have a hands-on approach. To that extent, classes will consist primarily of experiments, computer-based activities, interactive discussions, exploratory worksheets, and other cooperative learning group activities.

Intended Learning Outcomes

All sections of INQ 250 share a common set of learning outcomes related to the skills students will develop in this course. These outcomes are:

1. Students will be able to describe and apply scientific methodologies appropriate for the course's discipline and topic, including the ability to design and conduct simple experiments and to draw conclusions based upon data.

2. Students will be able to articulate how the course's perspective was reflected in the course content.

3. Students will be able to write about course topics clearly and effectively.

4. Students will be able to communicate effectively about the course topic in an oral format.

5. Students will be able to interpret quantitative information related to the course topic.

In this section of INQ 250, these common outcomes will be developed in specific assignments so that at the completion of this course, successful students will

1. Gain a better understanding of the scientific method by refining predictions based on experimental observations

2. Use the scientific method to devise their own experiment to further study motion

3. Practice communication skills by orally presenting their project findings to the class

4. Present their daily findings and project results in a well-organized written manner

5. Become familiar with computer-interfaced sensors

6. Demonstrate their ability to create, correctly analyze, and interpret graphical data

7. Possess a basic understanding of Newton's laws of motion and be able to express them in their own words

Attendance

Students are expected to attend every class. Attendance is checked at each meeting. Since this course uses a hands-on approach to learning, it is very important for each student to be present for every class. **If a student accumulates four absences during the semester, a warning letter will be sent. If the fifth absence occurs,** *for any reason,* **the student may be dropped from the course.**

Daily Assignments

Daily assignments incorporate several areas: lab work, class work, homework, and quizzes. Each assignment is worth 20 points, and all types of daily assignments are weighted equally.

Each student should record all lab work on **graph paper in their notebook**. Whenever lab work is graded, either the individual pages or the entire notebook may be submitted. When absent from class, the student is still responsible for the work and should copy the data and answer the questions immediately upon return to class.

Class work may be graded individually or as a group. Included in class work are daily questions concerning lab activities, class worksheets, and graphing activities. If a student is absent when a class assignment is graded, a zero is recorded. So it is important to be in class!

Homework is assigned often and is graded. Each assignment is due at the beginning of class on the date stated and is to be submitted individually. You may seek and receive additional assistance for each homework assignment without violating any academic integrity policies. If you are absent when an assignment is due, the assignment is still due at the beginning of class, and it can be submitted electronically or sent via another student.

Quizzes will be announced, and no makeup quizzes will be given. It is possible to schedule to take a quiz early if you are going to be absent for a college function, but arrangements for taking the quiz must be made two class periods before the absence will occur. Each quiz will be taken individually, and the work is subject to the college's academic integrity policies.

When calculating the daily assignment average for the semester, the *four lowest grades* will be dropped.

Makeup Exams

Makeup exams will be given only at the discretion of the instructor. It will be considered only in the event of **prior notification of the absence**. Otherwise, a missed exam results in the final exam counting an additional 20%.

Electronic Devices Usage Policy

Computers in the lab are networked, and you are required to log onto them with your username and password. **Do not save any work to the desktop**, because it will be erased when logging off the computer at the end of class. Save all work to your Z drive. Printing graphs will be necessary throughout the semester, but these pages printed from the printer in this room currently do not count against your total pages allotted by the college. **Computers, including laptops, are not to be used to check e-mail or access the Internet for personal reasons during class**. Also, MP3 players, cameras, and other personal devices are not to be used during class, except cameras may be helpful during project time. Personal laptops and calculators may be used as directed.

Out of courtesy to others, **all cell phones should be silenced** upon arrival to class and should be out of sight, preferably in a backpack or personal bag. This means that you are **to refrain from texting** while in class, since your cell phone will not be out of your backpack or personal bag.

Violation of this policy will result in a warning for the first offense, and the placing of the cell phone on the instructor's desk for any subsequent offenses.

MCSP Conversation Series

The Math/Computer Science/Physics professors will be presenting talks to Roanoke College students throughout the semester. The schedule will be posted in the lab and is located online at http://cs.roanoke.edu/MCSPSeries/. You are required to attend one session for the entire length of the talk and questioning time, listen attentively, and write a one-page summary paper that also includes your justified critique of the talk. **To receive credit for attending the talk, the written assignment is to be received within 7 days of that lecture.** Attending a talk and submitting a paper within the required 7 days will provide you with 5 extra points added to your exam score. Up to three lectures may be attended and extra credit given, provided the papers are submitted within the seven-day requirement. Failure to attend a lecture or submit an adequately written paper within the allotted time will result in no additional points being added.

Projects

During this semester, you will participate in two group projects. It is expected that each individual member of the group will share equally in the work. A document explaining the required elements of the project will be given to all students closer to the start of projects.

Grading

At the end of the semester, grades will be determined as follows:

Grade Determination
Daily assignments: 20%
2 unit exams: 25 % each
Group projects: 10% each
Final exam: 20%

Grading Scale
A: > 93, A−: 90−92.9, B+: 87−89.9,
B: 83−86.9, B−: 80−82.9, C+: 77−79.9,
C: 73−76.9, C−: 70−72.9, D+: 67−69.9,
D: 63−66.9, D−: 60−62.9, F: <60

Students with Special Academic Needs

If you are on record with the college's Special Services as having special academic or physical needs requiring accommodation, please meet with me during my office hours as soon as possible to discuss implementation of your requests. Testing accommodations must be arranged at least one week prior to each unit exam and the final exam.

Course Restrictions

Be aware that if you have received credit for any other higher-level physics courses at Roanoke College, you cannot receive credit for this course.

Food, Drink, and Tobacco Use

No food items should be brought into the lab, as the lab surfaces are not sanitized and food particles may damage the lab equipment. Bottled water may be brought into the lab as long as the bottle is capped when resting on the lab table. Chewing tobacco is not allowed in the lab.

Academic Integrity

The College academic integrity policies are vigorously enforced. All quizzes and exams are to be your individual work, without assistance from any other source. Projects and class activities are to be collaborative work between individuals within your group. Outside assistance may be sought on homework, but the work submitted for a grade must reflect your understanding of the material and not exact answers copied from another's work.

Week	Date	Topic	
1	31-Aug	Course Policies & Introduction	
	2-Sep	Making Measurements; Measurement Error; Graphs	
	5-Sep	Overview; The Measurement Process; Analyzing Motion	
2	7-Sep	Velocity & Speed; Position-Time Graphs	
	9-Sep	Velocity-Time Graphs	
	12-Sep	Developing a Hypothesis; Effects of a Push	
3	14-Sep	Acceleration	
	16-Sep	Forces & Mass	
	19-Sep	Forces & Mass	*Project A:* Project selection
4	21-Sep	Newton's Second Law	
	23-Sep	Newton's Second Law & Friction	*Project A:* Proposal due
	26-Sep	**Project A:** In-class data collection	
5	28-Sep		
	30-Sep		
	3-Oct	**Project A:** In-class data collection	
6	5-Oct		
	7-Oct	*How to Write an Abstract*	*Review for Exam A*
	10-Oct	**Project A:** Presentations	*Review for Exam A*
7	12-Oct	**Unit A Exam**	
	14-Oct	Forces Review	*Project A:* Abstract rough draft due
	17-Oct	*Fall Break (No class)*	
8	19-Oct		
	21-Oct		
	24-Oct	Floating, Sinking & Forces	
9	26-Oct	Buoyancy	
	28-Oct	Buoyancy	*Project A:* Abstract final draft due
	31-Oct	Archimedes Principle	

Week	Date	Topic	
10	2-Nov	Forces Exerted by a Gas	
	4-Nov	Hydraulic Lifts; Relation Between Pressure & Force	
	7-Nov	Measuring Pressure; Pressure & Wind I	*Project D:* Project selection
11	9-Nov	Pressure in a Fluid; Relation Between Pressure & the Buoyant Force	
	11-Nov	Barometers	*Project D:* Proposal due
	14-Nov	Bernoulli's Effect; Pressure & Wind II; Airfoils	
12	16-Nov	**Project D:** In-class data collection	
	18-Nov		
	21-Nov		
13	23-Nov	**Thanksgiving Break (no class)**	
	25-Nov		
	28-Nov	**Project D:** In-class data collection	
14	30-Nov		
	2-Dec	*Review for Exam D*	
	5-Dec	**Unit D Exam**	
15	7-Dec	**Project D:** Presentations	*Review for final exam*
	9-Dec	*Review for final exam*	*Project D:* Abstracts due
	12-Dec	*Final Exam 2:00* p.m.–5:00 p.m. **or**	
	14-Dec	*Final Exam 2:00* p.m.–5:00 p.m.	

Syllabus for Traveling Without Leaving: Global Sociology

INQ 260: "Traveling Without Leaving": Global Sociology

Spring 2011

Meeta Mehrotra
Office: 203 Trout Hall
Phone: 375–2420
E-mail: mehrotra@roanoke.edu

Class time: T/Th 8:30–10:00
Block: 9

Office Hours

Tuesday	Wednesday	Thursday
1:00–2:00	10:00–12:00	1:00–2:00
Or by appointment		

Course Description

Why do people take their shoes off when they enter a home in Japan? Why do some Egyptian women *choose* to wear the veil? Why are many marriages around the world still arranged by parents? These questions focus on practices that most Americans would find unusual. Yet studying these practices in a meaningful way will help students question their assumptions about others. Students will take a comparative global approach to study topics such as culture, gender relations, and family. This approach will facilitate a critical reflection on the central question this course focuses on: How do social forces shape the lives of individuals? Cross-cultural examinations of similarities and differences will help students investigate the ways in which social practices and institutions influence the trajectory of individual lives. Students will do a service-learning project that requires them to volunteer with an agency in the Roanoke Valley and reflect on their experiences in course assignments.

Learning Outcomes

Upon successful completion of this course, students will be able to

- Describe some of the global variations in cultural practices and social institutions
- Communicate effectively about global variations in cultural practices and social institutions in an oral format
- Describe the methodologies used by sociologists
- Explain how social forces shape individuals
- Write about the impact of social forces in their own lives clearly and effectively
- Articulate how the course's perspective (global) was reflected in the course content

Course Format

The course format consists of some lectures, extensive class discussions, and in-class activities. In addition, we will watch some films and may listen to guest speakers. I encourage you to participate actively in this course. My expectation is that as college students, you have an interest in and commitment to learning. This means that you are ready to work hard, come prepared to class, and tackle readings and assignments that you may consider difficult. It is your responsibility to do all the assigned readings *before* class and participate in class discussions. We will not go over all the assigned material in class; I expect you to keep up with the reading. I may call on students randomly to respond to assigned readings, so please come to class prepared.

Honest class discussion is an important part of this course; hence, everyone should be comfortable in class. Remarks that indicate a lack of respect for the feelings and comments of others, or remarks that are derogatory toward individuals or groups on the basis of their gender, race/ethnicity, sexual orientation, age, nationality, religion, beliefs, physical appearance, etc., will not be tolerated. (Please remember that we can disagree with each other without showing disrespect.)

Attendance Policy

Class attendance is crucial for this course. It is important that you be here in order to participate in class discussions, and also because I may change or add to the assigned readings, or assign in-class projects. You are responsible for anything that you missed in class. I will keep a record of attendance. **You are allowed to miss TWO classes (*whatever the reason*) during the term. After that, I will take 2 points off your *final grade* for every additional unexcused absence from class.** (Absences will be excused only if you are *required* to participate in a college-sponsored event or if there is a *severe* illness or other emergency in your immediate family; you have to provide *official* documentation for your absence to be excused. I retain the right to determine if an absence will be excused or not.) Please pay attention while I take roll to ensure that I mark your presence. If you are late, let me know at the end of class that you were there or you will be marked as absent on the roster. Please come to class on time. I will keep a record of your tardiness and will use it to assess borderline grades. Keep track of your absences. **I will NOT contact you (verbally or in writing) to warn you if you miss more than 2 classes.**

Academic Integrity

Students are expected to be familiar with the latest edition of the *Academic Integrity at Roanoke College* brochure and abide by the policies outlined in it. All necessary steps will be taken to enforce these policies to guarantee fairness to all students. You will be doing independent as well as shared projects in this course. Details about the nature and extent of sharing will be provided with each assignment. Please follow the instructions carefully to avoid even unintended violations of academic integrity. For individual and shared projects, be sure to cite all your sources. Review the section on plagiarism in the *Academic Integrity at Roanoke College* brochure and see me if you have any questions. Be aware of these regulations to avoid unintentional violations. Remember, ignorance is not bliss.

Cell phones, pagers, **laptops,** and other electronic devices must be turned off prior to entering the classroom. **The use of any electronic device during exams is strictly prohibited.** This includes iPods, PalmPilots, Pocket PCs, and BlackBerries. Any use of such devices during an exam will be considered a breach of academic integrity. Once you have begun an in-class exam, you cannot leave the room for *any reason* until you have turned your exam in to me (exceptions will be made at my discretion). If you leave the room, you will not be allowed to finish the exam.

Academic Services

The Writing Center @ Roanoke College, located in the Goode-Pasfield Center for Learning and Teaching in Fintel Library, offers writing tutorials for students working on writing assignments and projects in any field. Writers at all levels of competence may visit the Writing Center at any point in their process, from brainstorming to drafting to editing, and talk with trained peer writing tutors in informal, one-on-one sessions. I strongly encourage you to use their services. The Writing Center is open Sunday through Thursday from 4 p.m. to 9 p.m. beginning Sunday, January 23. You may simply stop in or schedule an appointment by going to www.roanoke.edu/writingcenter, where their schedule of writing workshops and creative writing playshops is also posted. You can also e-mail them at writingcenter@roanoke.edu or call 375–4949.

Subject Tutoring, located in the Goode-Pasfield Center for Learning and Teaching in Fintel Library, is available in various academic subjects such as Business and Economics, Foreign Languages, Lab Sciences, Math, and CPCS. Subject Tutoring is a nationally accredited program through the College Reading and Learning Association (CRLA) that requires all tutors to meet specific hiring criteria and complete 10 hours of training. Subject Tutoring is open Sunday through Thursday starting January 23 from 4 p.m. to 9 p.m. Their hours vary by subject, so be sure to visit their home page for a complete list of tutorial hours (www.roanoke.edu/tutoring) or call 375–4949.

The Office of Disability Support Services, located in the Goode-Pasfield Center for Learning and Teaching in Fintel Library, provides reasonable accommodations to students with identified disabilities. Although Roanoke College does not have special programs for students with disabilities, reasonable accommodations are provided based on the diagnosed disability and the recommendations of the professional evaluator. To be considered, students must identify themselves to the Office of Disability Support Services; specific current documentation of disabilities is required. For additional information, please contact Bill Tenbrunsel, associate dean, at 540–375–2247 or e-mail tenbruns@roanoke.edu.

If you are on record with the college's **Office of Disability Support Services** as having special academic or physical needs requiring accommodations, please meet with me during my regular office hours or schedule an appointment as soon as possible. We need to discuss your accommodations before they can be implemented. Also, please note that you have to contact me to make arrangements for extended time on exams and testing in a semiprivate setting **at least one week before** *every* **exam**.

Required Readings

1. Ferrante, Joan. 2011. *Sociology: A Global Perspective* (7th ed.). Belmont, CA: Wadsworth Cengage Learning.

2. Schneider, Linda, and Arnold Silverman. 2010. *Global Sociology: Introducing Five Contemporary Societies* (5th ed.). New York: McGraw-Hill.

3. Hacker, Diana. 2009. *A Writer's Reference* (6th ed.). Boston: Bedford/St. Martin's.

4. The following books and readings are on reserve at the library:
   a. Andersen, Margaret, Kim Logio, and Howard Taylor (Eds.). 2001. *Understanding Society.* Belmont, CA: Wadsworth.
   b. Johnson, Allan. 2001. "The Forest and the Trees." Pp. 6–13 in *Understanding Society,* edited by Margaret Andersen, Kim Logio, and Howard Taylor. Belmont, CA: Wadsworth.
   c. Goodwin, Jeff, and James Jasper (Eds.). 2001. *The Contexts Reader.* New York: W. W. Norton and Company.
   d. Weiss, Robert S. 2001. "In Their Own Words: Making the Most of Qualitative Interviews." Pp. 498–506 in *The Contexts Reader*, edited by Jeff Goodwin and James Jasper. New York: W. W. Norton and Company.
   e. Macionis, John J., and Nijole Benokraitis. 2004. *Seeing Ourselves: Classic, Contemporary, and Cross-Cultural Readings in Sociology* (6th ed.). Upper Saddle River, NJ: Prentice Hall.
   f. Velliquette, Anne M., and Jeff B. Murray. 2005. "The New Tattoo Subculture." Pp. 66–78 in *Mapping the Social Landscape: Readings in Sociology*, edited by Susan J. Ferguson. New York: McGraw-Hill.
   g. Dibiase, Rosemarie, and Jaime Gunnoe. 2005. "Gender and Culture Differences in Touching." Pp. 113–122 in *Sociology: Windows on Society*, edited by Robert H. Lauer and Jeanette C. Lauer. Los Angeles: Roxbury Publishing Company.
   h. Barnes, J. A. 1997. "A Pack of Lies: Towards a Sociology of Lying." Pp. 67–73 in *Sociology: Exploring the Architecture of Everyday Life*, edited by David M. Newman. Thousand Oaks, CA: Pine Forge Press.
   i. Friedman, Thomas L. 2005. *The World Is Flat* (updated ed.). New York: Farrar, Straus and Giroux.
   j. Foek, Anton. 2005. "Sweatshop Barbie: Exploitation of Third World Labor." Pp. 225–229 in *Sociology: Windows on Society*, edited by Robert H. Lauer and Jeanette C. Lauer. Los Angeles: Roxbury Publishing Company.
   k. Branigin, William. 1996. "Children for Sale in Thailand: Poverty, Greed Force Girls into Prostitution." Pp. 114–117 in *Ourselves and Others: The Washington Post Sociology Companion*, edited by Karen Hanson. Needham Heights, MA: Allyn and Bacon.

1. Fernea, Elizabeth W., and Robert A. Fernea. 2003. "A Look Behind the Veil." Pp. 126–132 in *Readings for Sociology*, edited by Garth Massey. New York: W. W. Norton and Company.

5. You may be assigned additional readings for your "Conversations and Reflections" project or the alternate project.

Evaluation Criteria and Grading Scale

1. *Exams.* There will be two exams, worth 20% each. Exams will consist of a combination of multiple choice, short answer, and essay questions and may be in-class or take-home exams. Exam 2 is not cumulative but will include some material from earlier sections of the course.

2. *Conversations and Reflections project.* For this project, you will volunteer for a minimum of 15 hours with client families of the Refugee and Immigration Services of the Roanoke Valley. In addition, you will keep a journal, write an application paper, and take part in a panel discussion about your work. This project is worth 40% of your final grade. Details about this assignment will be provided in a separate handout. An alternative to this project will be provided.

3. *Writing/research assignment.* For this assignment, you will be asked to do a short writing and/or research assignment involving creation of interview questions and other tasks. Details about this assignment will be provided in a separate handout. This assignment is worth 10% of your final grade.

4. *News summary and class participation.* The remaining 10% of your final grade will be based on a news summary and various in-class exercises, including a group presentation. On designated Thursdays, you will team up with one or more classmates to do an oral presentation on the norms, gender roles, mate selection, or other aspects of a country of your choice. Details about this presentation will be provided in a separate handout.

   Each of you will be responsible for summarizing the day's news (national and international) on one class day during the semester. Your summary should be **no more** than 5 minutes long. A sign-up sheet will be provided. Acceptable sources include print, television, radio, or online versions of the BBC (http://news.bbc.co.uk), National Public Radio, Radio IQ, the *New York Times*, and other reliable domestic and international news sources. You are encouraged to use news sources from the country of your choice. The in-class exercises will not be announced in advance.

The final break-up is as follows:

Exams	40% (20% each) of the final grade
Conversations and Reflections project	40%
Writing/research assignment	10%
Class participation	10%

Note: Please remember that **unexcused absences will affect your grade**. Please refer to the section on the attendance policy.

Makeup Policy

You will be allowed to make up exams only if there is a serious illness or an emergency in your immediate family and if you provide *official* documentation. You have to let me know of your anticipated absence **before** the exam. If you face a sudden emergency on the day of the exam, let me know before the exam: call me, send me an e-mail, or send a note with a friend. You will NOT be allowed to make up the exam unless you let me know in advance. *All makeup exams will be essay exams and will be scheduled before the next class meeting or as soon as possible, at my convenience.*

All take-home assignments should be completed and turned in on time. If you need an extension, let me know before the due date. If you hand me a late assignment without having asked for an extension, I shall deduct 10% from your score for each day it is late. Assignments that are more than 5 days late (without permission) will get a score of 0. All take-home assignments have to be typed (double-spaced) and *stapled*, and handed to me *by you in class*. Assignments slipped under my office door or into my mailbox or sent with friends (without prior approval) will be considered late (*even if they are turned in on the day they are due*). There will be *no makeup or extended time* for class participation exercises.

The following grading scale (expressed in percentages) will be used:

90–100 = A	(90–92 = A-; 93–100 A)
80–89 = B	(80–82 = B-; 83–86 = B; 87–89 = B+)
70–79 = C	(70–72 = C-; 73–76 = C; 77–79 = C+)
60–69 = D	(60–62 = D-; 63–66 = D; 67–69 = D+)
Less than 60 = F	

Tentative Schedule (Subject to Change)

Information on where to find reserve articles, denoted by an asterisk, is at the end of this syllabus.

Jan 18: INTRODUCTION

Jan 20: WHY DO WE NEED A GLOBAL PERSPECTIVE?
  Read: *Ferrante*: Chapter 1, pp. 2–11, 20–24
  Schneider and Silverman: Introduction: To the Student

Jan 25: WHY DO WE NEED A GLOBAL PERSPECTIVE?
  Read: *Ferrante:* Chapter 1, pp. 11–19; Chapter 2, pp. 26–39

Jan 27: WHY DO WE NEED A GLOBAL PERSPECTIVE?
  Read: *Reserve:* "The Forest and the Trees" by Johnson*

Feb 1: METHODS OF SOCIAL RESEARCH
  Read: *Ferrante*: Chapter 2, pp. 40–55

Feb 3: METHODS OF SOCIAL RESEARCH
  Read: *Reserve*: "The Promises and Pitfalls of Going into the Field" by
    Adler and Adler*
  "In Their Own Words: Making the Most of Qualitative Interviews" by
    Weiss*

Feb 8: METHODS OF SOCIAL RESEARCH

Feb 10: HOW DOES OUR CULTURE SHAPE US?
  Read: *Ferrante*: Chapter 3
  Reserve: "India's Sacred Cow" by Harris*

Feb 15: HOW DOES OUR CULTURE SHAPE US?
  Read: Schneider and Silverman:
    Japanese Culture (pp. 3–16)
    Mexican Culture (pp. 83)
    San Culture (pp. 129–146)
    Egyptian Culture (pp. 185–200)
    German Culture (pp. 255–268)

Feb 17: HOW DOES OUR CULTURE SHAPE US?
  Read: *Reserve:* "The New Tattoo Subculture" by Velliquette and Murray*
  "Gender and Culture Differences in Touching" by Dibiase and Gunnoe*
  "A Pack of Lies: Towards a Sociology of Lying" by Barnes*

Feb 22: HOW DOES OUR CULTURE SHAPE US?

Feb 24: EXAM I

Mar 1: THE IMPACT OF ECONOMIC FORCES
  Read: *Ferrante:* Chapter 11, pp. 298–315

Mar 3: THE IMPACT OF ECONOMIC FORCES
  Read: *Ferrante*: Chapter 8, pp. 220–226

Mar 5–13: Spring Break

Mar 15: THE IMPACT OF ECONOMIC FORCES
  Read: *Ferrante:* Chapter 8, pp. 198–220
  Schneider and Silverman:
      Social Inequality in Japan (pp. 46–57)
      Social Inequality and Conflict in Mexico (pp. 102–121)
      Social Inequality in Egypt (pp. 226–238)
      Inequality and Diversity in Germany (pp. 286–295)

Mar 17: THE IMPACT OF ECONOMIC FORCES
  Read: *Reserve*: "While I was Sleeping" by Friedman*
  "Sweatshop Barbie: Exploitation of Third World Labor" by Foek*
  "Children for Sale in Thailand: Poverty, Greed Force Girls into
      Prostitution" by Branigin*

Mar 22: THE IMPACT OF ECONOMIC FORCES

Mar 24: THE SOCIAL CONSTRUCTION OF GENDER
  Read: *Ferrante:* Chapter 10

Mar 29: THE SOCIAL CONSTRUCTION OF GENDER
  Read: *Schneider and Silverman:*
      Gender Roles in Japan (pp. 39–45)
      Gender Inequality Among the San (pp. 153–155)
      Culture and Gender Roles in Egypt (pp. 200–213)

Mar 31: THE SOCIAL CONSTRUCTION OF GENDER
  Read: *Reserve:* "A Look Behind the Veil" by Fernea and Fernea*

Apr 5: FAMILY: A CULTURAL UNIVERSAL?
  Read: *Ferrante:* Chapter 12, pp. 330–341
  Reserve: "Mate Selection and Marriage Around the World" by Ingoldsby*
  "Love, Arranged Marriage, and the Indian Social Structure" by Gupta*

Apr 7: FAMILY: A CULTURAL UNIVERSAL?
  Read: *Ferrante:* Chapter 12, pp. 341–364
  Schneider and Silverman:
      Social Structure and Group Life in Mexico (pp. 83–92)
      Social Structure and Group Life Among the San (pp. 146–153)
      Social Groups in Egyptian Life (pp. 213–219)

Apr 12: FAMILY: A CULTURAL UNIVERSAL?

Apr 14: FAMILY: A CULTURAL UNIVERSAL?

Apr 19: Presentations/panel discussion

Apr 21: Presentations/panel discussion

APR 28: EXAM II (8:30–11:30 a.m.)

Accessing Reserve Readings

A. *Articles on e-reserve:* From Fintel Library's home page, choose Course Reserves, then Search by Professor and choose the readings for IN260SO. The password is _____
   1. Johnson, Allan. "The Forest and the Trees."
   2. Weiss, Robert. "In Their Own Words: Making the Most of Qualitative Interviews."
   3. Velliquette, Anne, and Jeff B. Murray. "The New Tattoo Subculture."
   4. Dibiase, Rosemarie, and Jaime Gunnoe. "Gender and Culture Differences in Touching."
   5. Barnes, J. A. "A Pack of Lies: Towards a Sociology of Lying."
   6. Foek, Anton. "Sweatshop Barbie: Exploitation of Third World Labor."
   7. Branigin, William. "Children for Sale in Thailand: Poverty, Greed Force Girls into Prostitution."
   8. Fernea, Elizabeth, and Robert A. Fernea. "A Look Behind the Veil."
   9. Gupta, Giri Raj. "Love, Arranged Marriage, and the Indian Social Structure."

B. The following articles are in books on reserve, available at the circulation desk of Fintel Library. **At the desk, please ask for the author of the book, NOT the article**.

Article	Book	Page Nos.
"The Sociological Imagination" by C. Wright Mills	*Understanding Society,* edited by Margaret Andersen, Kim Logio, and Howard Taylor	Pp. 1–5
"The Promises and Pitfalls of Going into the Field" by Patricia Adler and Peter Adler	*The Contexts Reader,* edited by Jeff Goodwin and James Jasper	Pp. 490–497
"India's Sacred Cow" by Marvin Harris	*Seeing Ourselves: Classic, Contemporary, and Cross-Cultural Readings in Sociology* (6th ed.), edited by John J. Macionis and Nijole V. Benokraitis	Pp. 46–49

Article	Book	Page Nos.
"While I Was Sleeping" by Thomas Friedman	*The World Is Flat,* by Thomas L. Friedman (updated ed.)	Pp. 3–49
"Mate Selection and Marriage Around the World" by Bron Ingoldsby	*Seeing Ourselves: Classic, Contemporary, and Cross-Cultural Readings in Sociology* (6th ed.), edited by John J. Macionis and Nijole V. Benokraitis	Pp. 338–344

Syllabus for Elite Deviance: Crime in the Suites

INQ-260SOW-A: Elite Deviance: Crime in the Suites

Roanoke College—Spring 2010

MWF 8:30–9:30 a.m. (Block 1)—Trout 207

Diane V. Brogan
Phone: 375–2472
992–5886 (home)

Office: Trout 205
Office Hours: MWF 10:50–11:50 a.m. and by appt.
E-mail: dbrogan@roanoke.edu

COURSE DESCRIPTION

Drawing from the work of C. Wright Mills and the conflict perspective, this course utilizes a definition of elite deviance that refers to the criminal and deviant behaviors of those with power, privilege, and wealth in society, including both individuals and organizations within the corporate, governmental, and political realms. A "power elite" has emerged from these individuals and groups that has increasing exclusive access to economic and political power. Their deviant behaviors, referred to as "the higher immorality," are designed to increase power and profit and are often driven by institutionalized creeds such as "greed is good" and "business as usual."

Students are introduced to numerous case studies of white-collar crime and corporate and governmental deviance in order to analyze their historical treatment and to apply the theoretical perspectives that attempt to explain and understand the behavior. Using the sociological imagination as well as macro and micro levels of analysis, students will define the role of American values and the American dream in this social problem.

Students will examine society's differential response to elite deviance, which is often mediated by the actor's social class and the context of the behavior. Complex organizational hierarchies and processes provide protection leading to "elitist invisibility." Nonelite deviants or "street criminals" are more likely to be stigmatized despite the significant and often devastating consequences and social costs of elite deviance.

While the focus of the course is the case study, students will be introduced to other social science methods with particular attention to the efficacy of qualitative versus quantitative methods for this topic.

Intended Learning Outcomes

Upon successful completion of this course, students will be able to

- Identify the nature of elite deviance, as well as its social costs and consequences
- Analyze the role of power, privilege, and wealth in this social problem
- Critically evaluate the conditions and social arrangements that precipitate elite deviance and affect society's response to it
- Predict what social changes would be needed to significantly reduce the incidence of this behavior
- Synthesize, critique, and summarize material effectively in order to communicate more succinctly both verbally and in writing

Required Reading

Hacker, Diana. 2007. *A Writer's Reference*, 6th ed. Boston: Bedford/St. Martin's.
Shover, Neal, and John Paul Wright, eds. 2001. *Crimes of Privilege: Readings in White-Collar Crime.* New York: Oxford University Press.
Simon, David R. 2006. *Elite Deviance,* 8th ed. Needham Heights, MA: Pearson/Allyn and Bacon.

Students will also be required to read "The Promise" and "The Power Elite," both by C. Wright Mills, and "C. Wright Mills and Higher Immorality: Implications for Corporate Crime, Ethics, and Peacemaking Criminology" by John Wozniak. These articles will be made available in the Sociology Library on the first floor of Trout.

Course Format and Policies

Class meetings will consist primarily of class discussion and student presentation. The instructor will provide direction and facilitate discussion. All students are expected to participate in class discussions and exercises in order to more fully examine and apply course material. Guest speakers and the viewing of videos are planned for the same purpose. Students are required to do the assigned reading for each class *prior to* attending that class.

Regular class attendance is expected of all students; therefore, attendance will be taken and recorded. Each student is allowed two absences for whatever reason—illness, sporting event, lack of interest in class that day, etc. Each student is responsible for deciding between difficult choices of whether to attend class versus some other pressing event. Students are advised not to buy airline tickets or make other commitments with the intent of negotiating with the instructor. Since attendance is viewed as a critical component of the student's responsibility in this course, *each absence after two will result in a loss of 5 points from the final exam grade.*

Makeup examinations will be given only for the most extenuating circumstances, which involve a written medical excuse, a letter from the registrar, or other written documentation. Again, students are advised not to buy airline tickets or make other commitments with the hope that a makeup or early exam will be given. Exams will not be scheduled for your individual convenience.

Students are kindly requested to submit all papers in this course printed on both sides of the paper = reduce, reuse, recycle! ♻

Evaluation Criteria and Grading System

Writing Assignments. Students will be assigned *three separate writing assignments* during the course. These assignments will involve synthesis, analysis, and application regarding films, content from speakers or group discussions, and/or specific issues or questions from class material. Students will work in small groups where they will present their work and provide feedback to each other. Failure to be present for these group feedback sessions will result in additional point reduction from the grade assigned. Papers will be graded with equal attention to style of writing as well as argument and content. The *numerical average of the student's grades* on these assignments will constitute *40% of the final course grade.* All papers are to be submitted to SafeAssign by the class session they are due.

Note: Students are directed to ''Guidelines and Resources for Making a Sociology Presentation and Writing a Sociology Paper'' for guidance in preparing work for this class. The information is available on the Sociology Web site.

Class Participation. Each student will be evaluated and assigned a subjective grade by the instructor for his/her class participation. This grade will constitute *10% of the student's final grade*. **Evaluations of** class participation will be based primarily on the quality of the questions asked and answered by the student both in exchange with the instructor and other students as well as comments on course material. Quantity of comments will never outweigh quality of analysis, critique, and thought. Peer review forms and processes are included in this grade assessment.

Examinations. There will be two written examinations administered during this course. Each will be worth 100 points, and *each will constitute 25% of the final grade*.

Grading Scale.

100 to 90 = A	(91 to 90 = A−)
89 to 80 = B	(89 to 88 = B+) (81 to 80 = B−)
79 to 70 = C	(79 to 78 = C+) (71 to 70 = C−)
69 to 60 = D	(69 to 68 = D+) (61 to 60 = D−)
Below 60 = F	

ANY WORK SUBMITTED LATE (MEANING AFTER THE CLASS SESSION FOR WHICH IT IS DUE) WILL RECEIVE A LOSS OF 10 POINTS PER DAY FOR EACH DAY IT IS LATE. WORK NOT SUBMITTED TO SAFEASSIGN BY THE DUE DATE WILL RECEIVE A FAILING GRADE.

Academic Integrity

All students are expected to be familiar with and adhere to all of the policies outlined in *Academic Integrity at Roanoke College.* All necessary steps will be taken to enforce these policies in an effort to guarantee fairness for all students and to uphold the values embodied by this honor system. Any exceptions with regard to specific written or oral assignments will be discussed in class. Students should be diligent in their efforts to document sources used in all researched projects. Resources defining plagiarism are available and any students with questions should see the instructor. ***ALL PAPERS ARE TO BE SUBMITTED TO SAFEASSIGN BY THE DATE AND CLASS PERIOD THEY ARE DUE.***

No active beepers, cell phones, or other electronic devices are allowed during class meetings. Even the appearance of impropriety must be avoided and will not be tolerated.

Special Accommodations

If you are on record with the college's Special Services as having special academic or physical needs requiring accommodations, please meet with me during my regular office hours as soon as possible. We need to discuss your accommodations before they can be implemented. Also, please note that arrangements for extended time on exams and testing in a semiprivate setting must be made by you with me at least one week before EVERY exam. TESTS IN THIS COURSE ARE DESIGNED TO BE TAKEN DURING THE LENGTH OF TIME ALLOTTED FOR THE CLASS PERIOD. NO ADDITIONAL TESTING TIME WILL BE GIVEN WITHOUT A SPECIFIC STATEMENT OF ACCOMMODATIONS AS DESCRIBED IN THIS SECTION. If you believe you are eligible for accommodations but have not yet formally contacted Special Services, please call 375–2249 or drop by the Center for Learning and Teaching in Fintel Library.

Tentative Course Outline and Reading Assignments

All conditions of this syllabus are subject to change with adequate notice to students.

Date	Topics	Student's Responsibility (what you should have read or done for this class session)
1/11 (M)	Introduction to Course—syllabus, policies	
1/13 (W)	Academic Integrity, Hacker Handbook, ASA Format White Collar Crime Categories	Shover, p. 4 "White-Collar Criminality"
1/15 (F)	Sociological Concepts—Tools to Understand Elite Deviance in Social Context	Article: "The Promise"
1/18 (M)	Same as above	Article: "The Power Elite"
1/20 (W)	Same as above	
1/22 (F)	Library instruction by R. Heller—bring your laptop if you wish	

Date	Topics	Student's Responsibility (what you should have read or done for this class session)
1/25 (M)	Nature of Elite Deviance: Conditions and Consequences	Simon, chap. 1; Shover, p. 51: "Neglected Victims and Costs"
1/27 (W)	Same as above	Same as above
1/29 (F)	**Writing Assignment 1**:Researching the Power Elite. Group feedback (final draft due 2/3)	Bring your written assignment to class; prepare to workshop it
2/1 (M)	Elite Deviance and Higher Immorality	Simon, chap. 2
2/3 (W)	Same as above	Same as above
2/5 (F)	Video: *The Corporation*	
2/8 (M)	Same as above	
2/10 (W)	Same as above	
2/12 (F)	Discussion of video: Developing research questions	
2/15 (M)	Introduction to Sociological Research	Shover, p. 67: "White-Collar Victimization"; Shover, p. 87: "Victims of Fraud"
2/17 (W)	Same as above	Same as above
2/19 (F)	Corporate Deviance: Monopoly, Manipulation, Fraud	Simon, chap.3
2/22 (M)	Same as above	Same as above
2/24 (W)	Same as above	Same as above
2/26 (F)	**Exam 1**	
3/1 (M)	NO CLASS: SPRING BREAK	
3/3 (W)	NO CLASS: SPRING BREAK	
3/5 (F)	NO CLASS: SPRING BREAK	
3/8 (M)	Video: *Enron: The Smartest Guys in the Room*	
3/10 (W)	Continue video	
3/12 (F)	Discussion of video	
3/15 (M)	Corporate Deviance: Human Jeopardy	Simon, chap. 4; Shover, p. 156: "Fire in Hamlet"

Date	Topics	Student's Responsibility (what you should have read or done for this class session)
3/17 (W)	Same as above	Same as above
3/19 (F)	Political Deviance	Simon, chap. 7
3/22 (M)	Video: *The Most Dangerous Man in America: Daniel Ellsberg and the Pentagon Papers*	
3/24 (W)	Same as above	
3/26 (F)	**Writing Assignment 2:** Researching Political Deviance. Group feedback (final draft due 3/31)	Bring your written assignment to class; prepare to workshop it
3/29 (M)	Understanding Elite Deviance	Simon, chap. 8
3/31 (W)	Understanding Elite Deviance	Shover, p. 313: "Toward Understanding Unlawful Organizational Behavior" Shover, p. 210: "Organizational Culture & Organizational Crime" Shover, p. 222: "Profits, Pressure Corporate Law Breaking"
4/2 (F)	**NO CLASSES: GOOD FRIDAY**	
4/5 (M)	Understanding Elite Deviance	Shover, p. 329: "Characteristics and Sources of White-Collar Crime" Shover, p. 341: "Competition and Motivation to White-Collar Crime" Shover, p. 144: "Opportunity & Crime in the Medical Profession" Shover, p. 276: "Gender & Varieties of White-Collar Crime"

Date	Topics	Student's Responsibility (what you should have read or done for this class session)
4/7 (W)	Understanding Elite Deviance	" "
4/9 (F)	**Writing Assignment 3:** Student selects topic. Group feedback (final draft due 4/14)	Bring your written assignment to class; prepare to workshop it
4/12 (M)	Higher Immorality in an Era of Greed	Simon, chap. 9
4/14 (W)	Implications for the Future	Simon, Epilogue
4/16 (F)	Same as above	Shover, p. 381: "Prosecuting Corporate Crime"
4/19 (M)	Same as above	Article: "C. Wright Mills and Higher Immorality"
4/26 (M)	**FINAL EXAM: 8:30–11:30 a.m.**	

Syllabus for Does Gun Control Save Lives?

INQ 240—Statistical Reasoning: Does Gun Control Save Lives?

Spring 2011

Instructor: Dr. Chris Le   Trexler 270D   375-2347   clee@roanoke.edu

Course Description

Does gun control save lives? Such a politically charged question can be approached from many directions. In this course, students will learn the methodologies of modern statistics and use them to address the issue of measuring the effectiveness of gun control. Special attention will be given to the importance of being able to set aside politics, emotions, and preconceived notions in order to analyze a difficult question from a statistical point of view.

Overarching Goals

Students will be able to

- Apply their knowledge of statistics to analyze and assess the effectiveness of government regulations involving gun control.

- Compare and contrast different measures of "effectiveness" in regard to firearms regulations.

- Use statistics to identify biases in research involving gun control.

Ancillary Skill Goals

- Without interpretation, describe data both numerically and graphically.
- Apply their skills in using statistical software to break down and interpret large data sets.
- Understand the role of probability in statistical analysis.

Statistics Objectives

This course provides an inquiry-focused introduction to statistical method-ologies. Students will gain an understanding of how decision making is accomplished using modern statistical techniques. Topics include descriptive statistics, graphical methods, estimation, elementary probability, and statistical inferences; students will apply the techniques of data analysis to data sets and statistical studies.

Technology

For some sections of the course, students will need statistical software for calculations and graphics. Excel and Minitab are provided on college lab computers. Students will also need a scientific calculator.

Required Texts and Readings

- *Statistics: Concepts and Controversies*, 7th edition. Moore and Notz.
- *Guns, Gun Control, and Elections*. Harry Wilson.
- *A Writer's Reference* (6th ed.). Diana Hacker.

Attendance

Attendance is critical to the understanding of the material in the course; it is both required and expected. On each class day you will be marked as one of: prepared, present, absent, or unexcused absent.

- Prepared: You show your completed HW to the instructor on the way into class. Note: you cannot be marked prepared if you arrive late to class.
- Present: You may be physically in class, but your HW was not complete.
- Excused absent: Your absence is excused through prior notification of the instructor.
- Unexcused absent: Any absence that is not discussed with the instructor prior to the missed class is considered unexcused.

Unexcused absences may result in the lowering of the final grade. I will assume that if you accumulate 3 unexcused absences, you are not interested in completing the course and will drop you from the class. When absent, excused, or unexcused, you are responsible for all material covered in class. You will not be allowed to make up any work missed due to an unexcused absence.

Homework

Homework problems will be assigned and checked daily. Do not wait to start these until the night before the next class period.

Quizzes/Tests

You will not be able to procrastinate in this course. There will be 3 tests and at least 8 quizzes. Each week there will be either a quiz or a test. We will not spend time reviewing for these; the review is simply to complete the homework assigned. **NOTE**: There is a test on the Friday before break. Do not miss that day!

Writing/Oral Communication

While knowing statistics is important, it is useless if you cannot communicate the ideas and concepts you have learned and, more important, apply them to a controversial issue such as gun control. There are three writing assignments and one presentation throughout the semester. These are an important and significant component of the course. These assignments will push you to address issues from a statistical standpoint, argue your opinions, and improve your writing and communication skill.

Final Exam

The final exam will be cumulative, equally covering all material presented in the course.

Grading

Components of a student's grade will be weighted as follows:

Tests	40%
Homework/quizzes	10%
Personal writing	5%
Article analysis	5%
Group presentation	10%
Position paper	10%
Final exam	20%
	100%

A grade scale will be determined after final averages are computed, but will be no worse than the scale given below:

0	60	63	67	70	73	77	80	83	87	90	93
F	D−	D	D+	C−	C	C+	B−	B	B+	A−	A

Attendance and class participation will be considered when determining marginal and plus or minus grades.

Academic Integrity

Students are expected to adhere to the Academic Integrity policies of Roanoke College. All work submitted for a grade is to be your own work! No electronic devices other than calculators can be taken out during any class or testing period.

MCSP Conversations

The Math, Computer Science, and Physics Department offers a series of discussions that appeal to a broad range of interests related to these fields of study. These cocurricular sessions will engage the community to think about ongoing research, novel applications, and other issues that face our discipline.

Sessions are currently being scheduled, and all will be announced in advance.

Members of this class are invited to be involved with all of these meetings; however, participation in **at least one** of these sessions is mandatory. After attending, students will submit within one week of the presentation a one-page+ paper reflecting on the discussion. This should *not* simply be a regurgitation of the content but rather a personal contemplation of the experience.

Subject Tutoring

Student Tutoring, located in the Goode-Pasfield Center for Learning and Teaching in Fintel Library, is available in various academic subjects such as business and economics, foreign languages, lab sciences, math, and CPCS. Subject Tutoring is a nationally accredited program through the College Reading & Learning Association (CRLA) that requires all tutors to meet specific hiring criteria and complete 10 hours of training. Subject Tutoring is open Sunday through Thursday starting January 23 from 4 p.m. to 9 p.m. Our hours vary by subject, so be sure to visit our home page for a complete list of tutorial hours: www.roanoke.edu/tutoring. Questions? Call us at 375–4949.

The Office of Disability Support Services

Located in the Goode-Pasfield Center for Learning and Teaching in Fintel Library, this office provides reasonable accommodations to students with identified disabilities. Although Roanoke College does not have special programs for students with disabilities, reasonable accommodations are provided based on the diagnosed disability and the recommendations of the professional evaluator. To be considered, students must identify themselves to the Office of Disability Support Services; specific current documentation of their disabilities is required. Reasonable accommodations may include extended time for tests and examinations, testing in a semiprivate testing area, proctoring of examinations, use of interpreters, assistive technology, audio recording of lectures, and/or student note takers. For additional information please contact Bill Tenbrunsel, Associate Dean, at 540–375–2247 or e-mail tenbruns@roanoke.edu.

		Chapter from Moore	
Mon	Jan 17		**Writing** Preliminary Writing Assignment: Guns are _____. **Due** Friday, January 21
Wed	Jan 19	1	
Fri	Jan 21	2	
Mon	Jan 24	3	
Wed	Jan 26	4	
Fri	Jan 28	5	
Mon	Jan 31	6	
Wed	Feb 2	7	
Fri	Feb 7	9	
Wed	Feb 9	review	
Fri	Feb 11	**test 1**	
Mon	Feb 14	10	
Wed	Feb 16	11	
Fri	Feb 18	12	
Mon	Feb 21	13	**Writing** Analysis of an advocacy paper/article. Critique, 1–3 pages. **Due:** Friday, February 14
Wed	Feb 23	13	
Fri	Feb 25	14	
Mon	Feb 28	15	
Wed	Mar 2	review	

		Chapter from Moore	
Fri	Mar 4	**test 2**	
Spring Break			
Mon	Mar 14	16	
Wed	Mar 16	17	
Fri	Mar 18	18	
			Oral Communication
Mon	Mar 21	Presentations	Group presentations on chapters from Wilson text. 20 minutes, with audio/video
Wed	Mar 23	Presentations	
Fri	Mar 25	Presentations	
Mon	Mar 28	18	
Wed	Mar 30	19	
Fri	Apr 1	20	
Mon	Apr 4	review	
Wed	Apr 6	**test 3**	
			Writing
Fri	Apr 8	21	Formal Position Paper: ''We need more/less gun control.'' 3–5 pages. **Due:** Wednesday, April 23
Mon	Apr 11	21	
Wed	Apr 13	22	
Fri	Apr 15	22	
Mon	Apr 18	23	
Wed	Apr 20	23	
Fri	Apr 22	Good Friday, no class	
Mon	Apr 25	review	
Wed	Apr 27	2:00–5:00 p.m. Final Exam	

Syllabus for Statistics and Botany

Statistics and Botany

INQ 240N A/ Fall 2009

Instructor: Adam Childers/childers@roanoke.edu

Office: Trexler 270G

Phone: 540–375–2449

Office hours: 10:00 A.M.–11:00 A.M., Monday, Wednesday, Friday, 3:00 P.M.–4:30 P.M., Tuesday, Thursday, and by appointment.

Meeting Time: 12:00 P.M.–1:00 P.M., Monday, Wednesday, Friday

Meeting Place: 374 Trexler Hall

Required Texts

A First Course in Statistics, RC custom edition by McClave and Sincich

A Writer's Reference, RC custom edition by Diana Hacker

Additional Reading

Throughout the semester, we will also be consulting other texts and journal articles for meaningful data sets.

Course Objective

The objective of this course is to explore probability and statistics through botany. Topics such as how probability theory explains plant reproduction and how agricultural food is produced will be investigated. Through these topics, graphical representation of data, estimation, elementary probability, and statistical inference will be covered.

Intended Learning Outcomes

By the end of this course, students will be able to

- Use the methodologies of statistics to investigate a topic of interest and make decisions based on the results.
- Use the methodologies of statistics to design and carry out a simple statistical experiment.
- Use the methodologies of statistics to critique news stories and journal articles that include statistical information.
- Articulate the importance and limitations of using data and statistical methods in decision making.
- Express themselves clearly and effectively in writing using the concepts and language of statistics.
- Describe statistics and botany and its significance for understanding the natural world.
- Articulate the importance of the methodologies of statistics for understanding botany.

Homework

Homework will be assigned daily.

Quizzes and Tests

There will be a quiz or test each week of the semester. *Both will assess students' understanding of material covered in class, take-home readings, and homework assignments.*

Assignments and Projects

There will be two written assignments and one group project.

The first written assignment will be on relating probability theory to how plants reproduce. Each student will select a species and discuss its reproductive strategy in the context of probability theory.

The second written assignment will be on the economic viability and ethical acceptability of growing crops using genetically modified seeds. The report will include a statistical investigation of the issue.

Small groups will design and run experiments throughout the semester to determine how changes in a plant's environment affect germination, growth, and reproduction. The project will culminate with a written report and an oral presentation.

Final Exam

The final exam will be cumulative and will be Tuesday, December 8, 2:00 P.M.–5:00 P.M.

Grading

Grades will be assigned based on written assignments, quizzes, tests, and a final exam as follows:

Tests	45%
Quizzes and homework	10%
Assignments and Projects	30%
Final exam	15%

A *tentative* guideline for determination of grade will then be:

A	> 93	B	83– 86.9	C	73–76.9	D	63–66.9
A–	90–93	B–	80–82.9	C–	70–72.9	D–	60–62.9
B+	87–89.9	C+	77–79.9	D+	67–69.9	F	< 60

MCSP Conversation Series

Attending at least one MCSP conversation series event is required. Within one week of the lecture, a one-page reflection paper will be due and will count as a quiz grade. While attending only one event is required, students are encouraged to attend additional lectures.

Makeup Work

No makeup work will be accepted. Any excused work will be replaced by the final exam.

Attendance

Attendance is required, and acquiring more than two unexcused absences will result in a penalty. An absence is unexcused if it has not been discussed with and approved by the instructor before class.

Technology

Scientific calculators and the statistical program Minitab will be used throughout the semester in the classroom and on assignments. Cell phones and mp3 players are expected to be turned off before entering the class. Computers will be used in the classroom exclusively for academic purposes.

Academic Integrity System

The Roanoke College Academic Integrity System applies to all graded work in this course. Students are responsible for understanding and adhering to the Academic Integrity System. Among other things, the Academic Integrity System prohibits giving or receiving unauthorized aid, assistance, or unfair advantage on academic work.

The Office of Special Services

The Office of Special Services provides reasonable accommodations to students with identified disabilities. Although Roanoke College does not have special programs for students with disabilities, reasonable accommodations are provided based on the diagnosed disability and the recommendations of the professional evaluator. In order to be considered for special services, students must identify themselves to the Office of Special Services. Students are required to provide specific current documentation of their disability. Reasonable accommodations may include but are not limited to the following: extended time for test and examinations, testing in a semiprivate testing area, proctoring of examinations, use of interpreters, assistive technology, audio recording of lectures, and/or student note takers. For additional information please contact Pam Vickers, Special Services Coordinator, at 540–375–2247 or email vickers@roanoke.edu.

Course Schedule

The course schedule is given below, but note that is subject to change.

Content Topic: Exploring connections between plants, probability, and statistics

Wed	Aug 26		Introduction
Fri	Aug 28	1.1–1.6	Elements of Statistics, Types of Data, Collecting Data
Mon	Aug 31	2.1	Describing Qualitative Data
Wed	Sept 2	2.2	Graphical Methods
Fri	Sept 4	2.3, 2.4	Measures of Central Tendency; **Quiz 1**
Mon	Sept 7	2.5	Measures of Variability
Wed	Sept 9	2.6	Interpreting the Standard Deviation; **Project plan due**
Fri	Sept 11		**Test 1**

Content Topic: Investigating the connection between probability theory and plant reproduction

Mon	Sept 14	2.7, 2.8	Relative Standing, Outliers
Wed	Sept 16	3.1	Events, Sample Spaces, Probability
Fri	Sept 18	3.2, 3.3	Unions, Intersections, Complements; **Quiz 2**
Mon	Sept 21	3.3, 3.4	Additive Rule, Mutually Exclusive Events
Wed	Sept 23	3.5	Conditional Probability
Fri	Sept 25		**Test 2**
Mon	Sept 28	3.6	Multiplicative Rule, Independent Events
Wed	Sept 30	4.1, 4.2	Discrete Random Variables
Fri	Oct 2	4.3	Binomial Random Variable; **Quiz 3**

Content Topic: How statistics are used to grow food

Mon	Oct 5	4.3, 4.4	Binomial Continuous Variables, Normal Distribution
Wed	Oct 7	4.5	Normal Distribution: **WA 1 Due**
Fri	Oct 9	4.5	**Test 3**

Fall Break			
Mon	Oct 19	4.6, 4.8	Assessing Normality, Sampling Distributions
Wed	Oct 21	4.8	Sampling Distributions;
Fri	Oct 23	4.9	Central Limit Theorem; **Quiz 4**
Mon	Oct 26	6.1, 6.2	Hypothesis Testing: Large Sample
Wed	Oct 28	6.2, 6.3	Observed Significance Level
Fri	Oct 30		**Test 4**
Content Topic: Describing the behavior of plants statistically			
Mon	Nov 2	6.4	Hypothesis Testing: Small Sample
Wed	Nov 4	6.5	Hypothesis Testing: Proportions
Fri	Nov 6	7.2	Hypothesis Testing: Paired Differences; **Quiz 5**
Mon	Nov 9	10.1	Correlation; **WA 2 Due**
Wed	Nov 11	10.2	Regression
Fri	Nov 13	10.3	**Test 5**
Mon	Nov 16	10.5	Multiple Regression
Wed	Nov 18	5.1, 5.2	Confidence Intervals: Large Sample
Fri	Nov 20	5.2	Confidence Intervals: Large Sample; **Quiz 6**
Mon	Nov 23	5.3	Confidence Intervals **Thanksgiving Break**
Mon	Nov 30	5.5	Determining Sample Size
Wed	Dec 2		**Final Project Reports**
Fri	Dec 4		**Test 6**

REFERENCES

Allen, M. *Assessing Academic Programs in Higher Education.* San Francisco: Jossey-Bass, 2003.

Allen, M. *Assessing General Education Programs.* San Francisco: Jossey-Bass/Anker, 2006.

American Association of Colleges and Universities. "2009 Survey Talking Points." 2009. http://www.aacu.org/membership/2009survey talkingpoints.cfm.

American Association of Colleges and Universities. "Liberal Education and America's Promise." N.d. www.aacu.org/leap/vision.cfm.

Bartholomae, D. "Inventing the University." In M. Rose (ed.), *When a Writer Can't Write: Studies in Writer's Block and Other Composing Process Problems.* New York: Guilford Press, 1985.

Bean, J. C. *Engaging Ideas: The Professor's Guide to Integrating Writing, Critical Thinking, and Active Learning in the Classroom.* (2nd ed.) San Francisco: Jossey-Bass, 2011.

Clark, J. "Effective Pedagogy." In P. L. Gaston and others, *General Education and Liberal Learning: Principles of Effective Practice.* Washington, D.C.: American Association of Colleges and Universities, 2010.

Danielewizc, J., and Jordynn, J. "Teaching Writing in the Disciplines: A Genre-Based Approach." Workshop at Roanoke College, Feb. 13–14, 2009.

Diamond, R. M. *Designing and Assessing Courses and Curricula: A Practical Guide.* San Francisco: Jossey-Bass, 2008.

Eoyang, E. *Two-Way Mirrors: Cross-Cultural Studies in Glocalization*. Lanham, Md.: Lexington Books, 2007.

Ferren, A. "Intentionality." In P. L. Gaston and others, *General Education and Liberal Learning: Principles of Effective Practice*. Washington, D.C.: American Association of Colleges and Universities, 2010.

Gaff, J. "Avoiding the Potholes: Strategies for Reforming General Education." *Educational Record*, Fall 1980, 50–59.

Gaff, J., and Ratcliff, C. *Handbook of the Undergraduate Curriculum*. San Francisco: Jossey-Bass, 1997.

Gaston, P. "Imperatives for and Drivers of Change." In P. L. Gaston and others, *General Education and Liberal Learning: Principles of Effective Practice*. Washington, D.C.: American Association of Colleges and Universities, 2010a.

Gaston, P. "Principles of Strong General Education Programs." In P. L. Gaston and others, *General Education and Liberal Learning: Principles of Effective Practice*. Washington, D.C.: American Association of Colleges and Universities, 2010b.

Gaston, P. "Institutional Commitment." In P. L. Gaston and others, *General Education and Liberal Learning: Principles of Effective Practice*. Washington, D.C.: American Association of Colleges and Universities, 2010c.

Kellogg, R. T. "Training Writing Skills: A Cognitive Developmental Perspective." *Journal of Writing Research*, 2008, *1*(1), 1–26.

Klein, J. T. *Creating Interdisciplinary Campus Cultures: A Model for Strength and Sustainability*. San Francisco: Jossey-Bass, 2010.

Maki, P. "Assessment." In P. L. Gaston and others, *General Education and Liberal Learning: Principles of Effective Practice*. Washington, D.C.: American Association of Colleges and Universities, 2010.

Mantyla, T. "Optimizing Cue Effectiveness: Recall of 500 and 600 Incidentally Learned Words." *Journal of Experimental Psychology: Learning, Memory, an 1d Cognition*, 1986, *12*(1), 66–71.

McDonagh, P. "Engineering Better Engineers." *Concordia University Magazine*, Aug. 16, 2011. www.concordia.ca/now/what-we-do/teaching/20101018/engineering-better-engineers.php.

Menzel, P., and D'Aluisio, F. *What I Eat: Around the World in 80 Diets*. New York: Material World, 2010.

Rhodes, T. L. "Introduction." In P. L. Gaston and others, *General Education and Liberal Learning: Principles of Effective Practice*. Washington, D.C.: American Association of Colleges and Universities, 2010.

Roediger, H. L., III, and Karpicke, J. D. "Test-Enhanced Learning: Taking Memory Tests Improves Long-Term Retention." *Psychological Science*, 2006, *17*, 249–255.

Schilling, K. M., and Smith, D. "Alignment with the Majors." In P. L. Gaston and others, *General Education and Liberal Learning: Principles of Effective Practice*. Washington, D.C.: American Association of Colleges and Universities, 2010.

Suskie, L. *Assessing Student Learning: A Common Sense Guide.* (2nd ed.) San Francisco: Jossey-Bass, 2009.

Tewksbury, B., and Macdonald, R. H. *Designing Effective and Innovative Courses.* 2005. http://serc.carleton.edu/NAGTWorkshops/coursedesign/tutorial/.

Wabash Center of Inquiry for the Liberal Arts. "Overview of Findings from the First Year of the Wabash National Study of Liberal Arts Education." 2007. www.liberalarts.wabash.edu.

Walvoord, B. E. *Assessment Clear and Simple: A Practical Guide for Institutions, Departments, and General Education.* (2nd ed.) San Francisco: Jossey-Bass, 2010.

Wehlburg, C. M. "Integrated General Education: A Brief Look Back." In C. M. Wehlburg (ed.), *Integrated General Education.* New Directions for Teaching and Learning, no. 121. San Francisco: Jossey-Bass, 2010.

Zull, J. *The Art of Changing the Brain.* Sterling, Va.: Stylus, 2002.

INDEX

Also available from Jossey-Bass and AAC&U

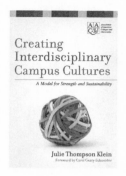

Creating Interdisciplinary Campus Cultures
A Model for Strength and Sustainability

Julie Thompson Klein

Cloth
ISBN 978-0-470-55089-2

"Klein's analysis shows convincingly that from research in the sciences to new graduate-level programs and departments, to new designs for general education, interdisciplinarity is now prevalent throughout American colleges and universities .... Klein documents trends, traces historical patterns and precedents, and provides practical advice. Going directly to the heart of our institutional realities, she focuses attention on some of the more challenging aspects of bringing together ambitious goals for interdisciplinary vitality with institutional, budgetary, and governance systems. A singular strength of this book, then, is the practical advice it provides about such nitty-gritty issues as program review, faculty development, tenure and promotion, hiring, and the political economy of interdisciplinarity .... We are proud to partner with Jossey-Bass in publishing this important study, and we know that readers everywhere will find it simultaneously richly illuminating and intensively useful."

—from the Foreword by Carol Geary Schneider, president,
Association of American Colleges and Universities

"Klein reveals how universities can move beyond glib rhetoric about being interdisciplinary towards pervasive full interdisciplinarity. Institutions that heed her call for restructured intellectual environments are most likely to thrive in the new millennium."

—William H. Newell, professor, Interdisciplinary Studies, Miami University,
and executive director, Association for Integrative Studies

"In true interdisciplinary fashion, Julie Klein integrates a tremendous amount of material in this book to tell the story of interdisciplinarity across the sciences, social sciences, and humanities. And she does so both from the theoretical perspective of 'understanding' interdisciplinarity and from the practical vantage of 'doing' interdisciplinarity. This book is a must-read for faculty and administrators thinking about how to maximize the opportunities and minimize the challenges of interdisciplinary programming on their campuses."

—Diana Rhoten, director, Knowledge Institutions Program,
and director, Digital Media and Learning Project, Social Science Research Council